Michael M. Dediu

J. R. Lucas

Philosopher on a creative parallel with

Plato

An American viewpoint

DERC Publishing House
Tewksbury (Boston), Massachusetts, U. S. A.

Copyright ©2016 by Michael M. Dediu

All rights reserved

Published and printed in the
United States of America

Library of Congress Control Number: 2016906560

Dediu, Michael M.

J. R. Lucas – philosopher on a creative parallel with Plato
An American viewpoint

ISBN-13: 978-1-939757326

1-3316044601
XX2343
04657D
25R68TRM
1-1IUACF7

Preface

Philosophy (in Greek means love of wisdom), mostly considered as a noble academic discipline, means the study of the fundamental principles and ideas of knowledge, truth, real world, proper behavior, values, and existence, based on logical reasoning. Some important personalities give their own interpretations: Protagoras (490 BC – 420 BC) – "Man is the measure of all things"; Socrates (470 BC – 399 BC) - "There is only one good, knowledge, and one evil, ignorance"; Aristotle (384 BC – 322 BC) - "We are what we repeatedly do. Excellence, then, is not an act, but a habit"; René Descartes (1596 – 1650) – "Cogito, ergo sum" (I think therefore I am); Bishop George Berkeley (1685 – 1753) - "Esse est percipi" (To be is to be perceived); Bertrand Russell (1872 – 1970) - "Science is what you know. Philosophy is what you don't know".

Plato (428 BC – 347 BC) was one of the greatest minds in human history, and he is the founder of the western philosophy: "What is at issue is the conversion of the mind from the twilight of error to the truth, which climb up into the real world which we shall call true philosophy".

J. R. Lucas, FBA, University of Oxford, is a mathematician, inventor, and one of the most distinguished philosophers of our time, who is a disciple of Plato, and who brings numerous new ideas in philosophy.

In this book, for the general public, we chronologically present happenings from Lucas' and Plato's lives, as well as many other interesting events and facts, and include many writings of Lucas, as well as comments about Lucas.

The wealth of the ideas from Lucas' books, having as roots Plato's books, represent a valorous contribution to our philosophical and cultural heritage, and will remain as a powerful testimony for the future generations.

Michael M. Dediu, Ph. D.

Boston, U. S. A., 20 April 2016

Michael M. Dediu is also the author of these books (which can be found on Amazon.com):

1. Aphorisms and quotations – with examples and explanations
2. Axioms, aphorisms and quotations – with examples and explanations
3. 100 Great Personalities and their Quotations
4. Professor Petre P. Teodorescu – A Great Mathematician and Engineer
5. Professor Ioan Goia – A Dedicated Engineering Professor
6. Venice (Venezia) – a new perspective. A short presentation with photographs
7. La Serenissima (Venice) - a new photographic perspective. A short presentation with many photos
8. Grand Canal – Venice. A new photographic viewpoint. A short presentation with many photos
9. Piazza San Marco – Venice. A different photographic view. A short presentation with many photos
10. Roma (Rome) - La Città Eterna. A new photographic view. A short presentation with many photos
11. Why is Rome so Fascinating? A short presentation with many photos
12. Rome, Boston and Helsinki. A short photographic presentation
13. Rome and Tokyo – two captivating cities. A short photographic presentation
14. Beautiful Places on Earth – A new photographic presentation
15. From Niagara Falls to Mount Fuji via Rome - A novel photographic presentation
16. From the USA and Canada to Italy and Japan - A fresh photographic presentation
17. Paris – Why So Many Call This City Mon Amour - A lovely photographic presentation
18. The City of Light – Paris (La Ville-Lumière) - A kaleidoscopic photographic presentation
19. Paris (Lutetia Parisiorum) – the romance capital of the world - A kaleidoscopic photographic view
20. Paris and Tokyo – a joyful photographic presentation. With a preamble about the Universe

21. From USA to Japan via Canada – A cheerful photographic documentary
22. 200 Wonderful Places, In The Last 50 Years – A personal photographic documentary
23. Must see places in USA and Japan - A kaleidoscopic photographic documentary
24. Grandeurs of the World - A kaleidoscopic photographic documentary
25. Corneliu Leu – writer on the same wavelength as Mark Twain. An American viewpoint
26. From Berkeley to Pompeii via Rome – A kaleidoscopic photographic documentary
27. From America to Europe via Japan - A kaleidoscopic photographic documentary
28. Discover America and Japan - A photographic documentary

Michael M. Dediu is the editor of these books (also on Amazon.com):

1. Sophia Dediu: The life and its torrents – Ana. In Europe around 1920
2. Proceedings of the 4th International Conference "Advanced Composite Materials Engineering" COMAT 2012
3. Adolf Shvedchikov: I am an eternal child of spring – poems in English, Italian, French, German, Spanish and Russian
4. Adolf Shvedchikov: Life's Enigma – poems in English, Italian and Russian
5. Adolf Shvedchikov: Everyone wants to be HAPPY – poems in English, Spanish and Russian
6. Adolf Shvedchikov: My Life, My Love – poems in English, Italian and Russian
7. Adolf Shvedchikov: I am the gardener of love – poems in English and Russian
8. Adolf Shvedchikov: Amaretta di Saronno – poems in English and Russian
9. Adolf Shvedchikov: A Russian Rediscovers America
10. Adolf Shvedchikov: Parade of Life - poems in English and Russian
11. Adolf Shvedchikov: Overcoming Sorrow - poems in English and Russian
12. Sophia Dediu: Sophia meets Japan
13. Corneliu Leu: Roosevelt, Churchill, Stalin and Hitler: Their surprising role in Eastern Europe in 1944
14. Proceedings of the 5th International Conference "Computational Mechanics and Virtual Engineering" COMEC 2013
15. Georgeta Simion – Potanga: Beyond Imagination: A Thought-provoking novel inspired from mid-20th century events
16. Ana Dediu: The poetry of my life in Europe and The USA
17. Ana Dediu: The Four Graces
18. Proceedings of the 5th International Conference "Advanced Composite Materials Engineering" COMAT 2014
19. Sorin Vlase – Mechanical Identifiability in Automotive Engineering
20. Sophia Dediu: Chocolate Cook Book: Is there such a thing as too much chocolate?

21. Gabriel Dima – The Evolution of the Aerostructures – Concept and Technologies

22. Proceedings of the 6th International Conference "Computational Mechanics and Virtual Engineering" COMEC 2015

Table of Contents

Preface 3
Table of Contents 9
Chapter 1: Young Lucas 11
Chapter 2: Lucas at Durham 30
Chapter 3: Lucas at Winchester 42
Chapter 4: Lucas at Oxford 84
Chapter 5: Lucas philosopher 152
Chapter 6: Lucas inventor 161
Chapter 7: Foreign Expeditions 180
Chapter 8: Autobiography of Old England 202

J. R. Lucas – philosopher on a creative parallel with Plato

Chapter 1: Young Lucas

1929. It was a nice and warm Tuesday, June 18th, 1929, and, while in London, during a speech, Charles G. Dawes (1865 – 1951, the 30th Vice President of the United States (1925 – 1929, under President Calvin Coolidge (1872 – 1933)), co-winner of the Nobel Peace Prize in 1925), in his new post as the American Ambassador (under 31st U.S. President Herbert Hoover (1874 – 1964, President 1929 – 1933)) to the United Kingdom (more precisely, to the Court of St. James's (which is the royal court for the Sovereign of the United Kingdom (George V (1865 – 1936, King 1910 – 1936, had 6 children)), named after St. James's Palace, but the title of the Court is transferred to the location where the Sovereign currently resides), 1929 – 1931), was calling for a naval disarmament conference (nice idea, just 10 years before World War II), the wife of Reverend Egbert de Grey Lucas (a Church of England (Episcopalian) clergyman who became Archdeacon of Durham; his mother was Kate Alman Smart, an Australian (her grandfather was a convict, sentenced at Lancaster in 1809, but her father T. W. Smart was a member of legislative council, and then a State Treasurer)), Mrs. Joan Mary Lucas (she had a sister, who will have two girls, Priscilla and Evelyn Dobbs; this sister will also be John's Godmother), gave birth in London to a little baby - John Randolph Lucas. He was the second child and elder son, and he was baptized John Randolph, in Salisbury Cathedral (120 km southwest of London, 15 km south of the prehistoric stone circle at Stonehenge, started 1220, very ornate, has a 123 m spire, a working 14th-century clock, and an original copy of the Magna Carta (1215)), by his grandfather, the Right Reverend John Randolph, Dean of Salisbury and formerly Bishop of Guildford (40 km southwest of London).. John's father was Vicar of the Ascension, Lavender Hill (in Battersea, South West London, 4 km south of Buckingham Palace). Until he married, he had been Winchester College Missioner, at St. John's Rudmore, Portsmouth (100 km southwest of London, on the south coast of England, on Portsea Island).

Reverend Egbert de Grey Lucas, the father of J.R. Lucas, around 1950.

Mrs. Joan Mary Lucas, the mother of J.R. Lucas, around 1925.

59 years later, from 27 August to 27 September 1988, Lucas writes for the British Academy:
"I was born in London on June 18th, 1929, the second child and elder son of the Reverend Egbert de Grey Lucas and Joan Mary his wife, and was baptized John Randolph, in Salisbury Cathedral

by my grandfather, the Right Reverend John Randolph, then Dean of Salisbury and formerly Bishop of Guildford. My Godparents were General C.C. Lucas, my uncle, M.J. Rendall, formerly Headmaster of Winchester, and Frances Evelyn Randolph (subsequently Mrs. J.H. Dobbs), my aunt.

My father was at that time Vicar of the Ascension, Lavender Hill. Until he married, he had been Winchester College Missioner, at St. John's Rudmore, Portsmouth. In 1930 (I think) he moved to St. Nicolas', Guildford, which is the first place I remember. In 1939 he became Archdeacon of Durham, and we lived in The College (i.e. the Close) Durham, until he retired in 1953, when we moved to Randolph's Steeple, Aston, Oxon, which my mother had recently inherited from her uncle. In his retirement he was Wiccamical Prebend of Chichester Cathedral until his death in 1958. My mother continued to live there and died in 1982.

My father and mother had four children, two sons and two daughters. My elder sister, Ann Rachel, was four years older, younger sister Sarah Kate eighteen months younger, and my brother, Paul de Neufville, four years younger. I can just remember waiting on the landing with Ann and hearing Paul's first cries.

The Rectory of St. Nicolas was a large late Victorian house, at 77 Portsmouth Road, with a large garden. After having been very hard up at The Ascension, my father and mother were relatively well off for a clerical family, but noticeably poorer than many of the parishioners, a number of whom gave the Rector's children generous Christmas presents. We had a cook, a succession of nursemaids and central heating, but there was a slight sense of financial worry in the background. I remember one occasion when the House Account was found to be 30 pounds overdrawn, which caused great alarm, and was finally attributed in part to having bought Devonshire cream when my Godfather, Monty Rendall had come to stay.

External events did not impinge very much in my early life. I just remember the General Election of 1935. The Conservative candidate was Sir John Jarvis, the Labour candidate a Mr. Campbell. I asked about the posters, and was given very firmly to understand, perhaps by a nursemaid or perhaps by our governess, that the Conservatives were good and Labour Bad: who then, I wondered, would vote for Mr. Campbell? Some of the people who worked on the railway, I was told; and immediately began to entertain a disloyal approbation of Mr. Campbell, being already fanatically keen on trains, having a working knowledge of all the local lines and a strong desire to be an engine-driver when I grew up. There was much worry about unemployment. I remember a huge block of coal exhibited in one of the streets, which was to be won by the person who most accurately guessed its weight, the proceeds to go to miner's relief. Sometimes men would come to the door to ask for work, and my father would give them 5 pounds to dig dandelions out of the lawn. The servants said darkly that the tramps put signs on the gate to tell others that we were a soft touch. I remember also – and I think this was quiet early on, 1934 or 1935 – being told by a nursemaid that toys made in Germany were bad.

Much the greater part of my early life was occupied in playing, sometimes with my brother and sisters, often by myself, being taken for walks, being inserted into clothes by nurses and female relatives, and in wondering. I remember lying outside the house on my sixth birthday, looking up at the sky and realizing that I should never be five again, and rather wishing that it were not the case that the past was irrevocable. I informed my brother on a hot thundery summer's day that everything was made of electricity: he, aged two, was somewhat unreceptive, but I made him repeat it after me until I was satisfied that the lesson had stuck.

There were electric trains at Guildford, and towards the end of the 1930s the mainline was also electrified. I was fascinated. I thought that electric motors ought to work like a mill wheel, with a stream of electrons coming out of the wire like a hose, and pushing the armature round by impulse."

Now just a few details: the son of a Church of England clergyman, and an Anglican himself, Lucas describes himself as "a dyed-in-the-wool traditional Englishman." He and Morar Portal have four children, among them Edward Lucas, International Editor of *The Economist*.

Lucas and his wife live in East Lambrook, Somerset, in southwest of England, 185 km southwest of London, 135 km southwest of Oxford, and 55 km south of Bristol, near the Crewkerne railway station (12 km south of East Lambrook), located in Misterton, 211.5 km from London Waterloo Station, on the West of England Main Line to Exeter (60 km southwest of East Lambrook).

Lucas has two sons, Edward and Richard, and two daughters, Helen and Deborah.

Lucas has a granddaughter, Antonia, a god-daughter in Alice Springs (a remote town in the center of Australia, 2,000 km northwest of Sydney), and a niece, Ruth Lucas, also in Australia, on her way to Perth (1829, a city on the south part of the west coast of Australia, where the Swan River meets the southwest coast, 3,500 km west of Sydney).

Much later, in February 2010 Professor Robin Attfield drove from Cardiff (port city on the south coast of Wales, on the River Taff at the Severn Estuary, 200 km west of London) to visit John and his wife in their village home in rural Somerset (60 km south of Cardiff, across the Bristol Channel), and to discuss philosophy.

Acknowledgement: I want to thank Professor Robin Attfield for his kind and prompt help.

At that time Prime Minister was Ramsay MacDonald (1866 – 1937, PM 1929 – 1935, FRS (Fellow of the Royal Society (1660, motto: Nullius in verba (Take nobody's word for it)))), Chancellor of the University of Oxford (1096) was Edward Grey (1862 – 1933, Chancellor (1928 – 1933)), and President of the British Academy (1902) was H. A. L. Fisher (1865 – 1940, President 1928–1932, FRS). When John was just a little over 2 months old, on August 20, 1929, the first transmissions of John Logie Baird's (1888 – 1946, engineer) experimental 30-line television system was done by the British Broadcasting Corporation (founded in 1922), and when he was a little over 4 months old, on Thursday October 24, 1929, began the Wall Street Crash of 1929, which is considered the beginning of the 10-year Great Depression that affected all Western industrialized countries.

Shakespeare's quote: *Love all, trust a few, do wrong to none.*

428 BC. About 2,357 years ago, around 428 BC, Plato (originally named Aristocles) was born in Classical Athens, Greece, his father being Ariston of the deme Collytus (c. 469 BC – c 424 BC, son of Aristokles, direct descendant of Solon's (640 BC – 558 BC, Athenian statesman and poet) brother Exekestiades), and mother Periktione, an aristocratic and influential family, and it seems Plato was expected to pursue a career in politics. His interests, however, tended more toward the arts and, in his youth, he wrote plays and, perhaps, poetry. When he was in his late teens, or early twenties, he heard Socrates (c. 470 BC – 399 BC, 42 years older than Plato) teaching in the market, and abandoned his plans to pursue a literary career as a playwright; he burned his early work and devoted himself to philosophy. Plato had two older brothers (Adeimantus and Glaucon), who both feature famously in Plato's dialogue "Republic", and a sister Potone.

At that time there was the Peloponnesian War (431 BC – 404 BC), between Athens with its empire and the Peloponnesian League led by Sparta. Pericles (495 BC – 429 BC) died one year before Plato's birth, and Cleon (c 485 BC – 422 BC) was the leader of Athens.

Socrates' quote: *True wisdom comes to each of us when we comprehend how little we understand about life, ourselves, and the world around us.*

1930. When little John was one year old, on June 18, 1930, beginning to walk a little bit, his father Reverend E. de G. Lucas, who had been a slum priest in South West London, moved to be Rector of St Nicolas Parish Church, Guildford (40 km southwest of London). The Rectory of St. Nicolas was a large late Victorian house, at 77 Portsmouth Road, with a large garden.

Prof. Dr. Paul Moldenhauer (1876 – 1947) resigned as German finance minister, starting the many changes and turbulences which affected Germany. On January 15, 1930, the Moon moved into its perigee (nearest point to Earth), at the same time as its fullest phase of the Lunar Cycle. This is the closest moon distance at 356,397 km in recent memory, and the next one will be 327 years from this day, on January 1, 2257, at 356,371 km. On 28 May, 1930, the BBC Symphony Orchestra is formed as a permanent full-scale ensemble, under the directorship of Adrian Boult (1889 – 1983). It gives its first concert on 22 October 1930 at the Queen's Hall (1893 – 1941), London (settled by Romans, during the 4th Emperor of the

Roman Empire, Claudius (10 BC – 54, Emperor 41 - 54), circa 43, as Londinium).

Shakespeare's quote: *Brevity is the soul of wit.*

427 BC. Going back 2357 years, to 427 BC, when little Plato was circa one year old, the Roman Republic (509 BC – 27 BC) was 82 years old, the Greek philosopher and Sophist Protagoras (480 BC – 411 BC) was 53 years old, and the Greek geometer Hippocrates of Chios (c. 470 BC – c 410 BC) was 43 years old. Sparta's King Archidamus II dies and is succeeded by his son Agis II. The Greek historian, soldier, mercenary and an admirer of Socrates, Xenophon, is born (d. 354 BC, at 73).

Socrates' quote: *Worthless people live only to eat and drink; people of worth eat and drink only to live.*

1931. Little John is 2 years old, walks, begins to talk, and on February 1st Boris Yeltsin is born (President of Russia, d. 2007), on March 2nd Mikhail Gorbachev is born (President of the Soviet Union, recipient of the Nobel Peace Prize), on May 1st the construction of the Empire State Building is completed in New York City. On June 3 Raul Castro is born (President of Cuba), on June 5, German Chancellor Dr. Heinrich Brüning (1885 – 1970, Chancellor 1930 - 1932) visits London, where he warns the British Prime Minister Ramsay MacDonald that the collapse of the Austrian banking system, caused by the bankruptcy of the *Creditanstalt*, has left the entire German banking system on the verge of collapse. On October 18 the American inventor Thomas Edison passed away at 84.

Milton's quote: *The superior man acquaints himself with many sayings of antiquity and many deeds of the past, in order to strengthen his character thereby.*

426 BC. Little Plato is around 2 years old and the Athenian leader Cleon and the Athenian general Demosthenes revitalize the city's military and naval forces. The Spartan general Eurylochus is killed during the Battle of Olpae (a fortress on the Ambracian gulf (Ionian Sea), 250 km northwest of Athens) by the naval forces under Demosthenes.

Socrates' quote: *Employ your time in improving yourself by other men's writings, so that you shall gain easily what others have labored hard for.*

1932. Little John is 3 years old, grows fast, plays a lot, and sometimes his parents took him, with their 5 years old car, on a Roman road, near Salisbury (120 km southwest of London, 15 km south of the prehistoric stone circle at Stonehenge, with an ornate 13th-century cathedral (which has a 123 m spire, a working 14th-century clock, and an original copy of the Magna Carta (1215))), where John's grandfather, from the mother side, was Dean, or Chichester, and he had a holiday house. Roman roads were very straight, and John's father was running at a speed between 45 and 55 mi/h. On those flat Roman roads the car once or twice went up to 60 mph.

At this time there are terrible purges done by Stalin in the Soviet Union (in the 1930s). There is a unique diary kept by Ivan Maisky (1884-1975), the Soviet ambassador to London between1932 and 1943. In this capacity he was able to witness and record the drift to war throughout the 1930s: appeasement, culminating in the Munich Agreement, the negotiations on the signature of the Molotov-Ribbentrop Pact, the battle for Britain, Churchill's rise to power, and the events leading to the German invasion of the Soviet Union. Then the forging of the Grand Alliance and the major debate between the Allies concerning the opening of the second front and the post war arrangements.

The President of the British Academy (1902) was John William Mackail (1859 – 1945, President 1932 – 1936, a scholar of Virgil (Publius Vergilius Maro, 70 BC in Cisalpine Gaul, Roman Republic – 19 BC in Brundisium, Roman Empire, very famous poet)). The positron (positive electron, the first known antiparticle of the electron) was discovered and photographed by the Nobel Laureate American Physicist Carl David Anderson (1905 – 1991). British Broadcasting Corporation (BBC) begins experimental regular TV broadcasts, and on December 19th begins transmitting overseas. On November 1st, Wernher von Braun (1912 – 1977), only 20 years old, was named the head of the German liquid-fuel rocket program. On November 8th, Franklin D. Roosevelt (1882 – 1945) was elected the 32nd President of the United States.

Milton's quote: *A good book is the precious lifeblood of a master spirit.*

425 BC. Little Plato is around 3 years old and Artaxerxes I, (circa 490 BC – 425 BC, the fifth King of Persia 465 BC – 425 BC, born in the reign of his grandfather Darius I (550 BC – 486 BC, King 522 BC – 486 BC)), Achaemenid king of Persia, dies, and is succeeded by his son Xerxes II (King for 45 days). The Athenian leader Cleon and the Athenian general Demosthenes have several victories over Sparta. Euripides' (480 BC – 406 BC) play Hecuba is performed. Herodotus of Halicarnassos, Dorian Greek historian (b. 484 BC), passes away at 59.

Plato's quote: *Access to power must be confined to those who are not in love with it.*

1933. Little (or Master) John is 4 years old, runs and talks. His father buys a Humber car fabricated on December 5th, 1927, at the Humber factory in Coventry (30 km east from Birmingham), and the car was baptized on April 24th, 1928, when it was first licensed, and bought by the Misses Peaks, who lived in Guildford.

The German president Paul von Hindenburg appoints Hitler (1889-1945) as chancellor, and 2 days later he dissolves the Parliament. On February 8th in the U. S., the first flight of all-metal Boeing 247 takes place, and just one day before Corneliu is 7 months old, the Congress repeals the alcohol Prohibition law. On March 6th Poland occupies the free city Danzig (Gdansk). Corneliu is a little over 8 months old and very happy, but his parents hear very bad news: German Reichstag grants Hitler dictatorial powers, and soon after Japan leaves the League of Nations. On May 10th Paraguay declares war on Bolivia. On August 30th Air France forms. In Cuba, Batista (1901-1973) becomes dictator at 32. On November 16, Brazilian President Getulio Vargas (1883-1954) declares himself dictator, and the United States recognizes the Soviet Union, establishes diplomatic relations and opens trade. To celebrate their recognition by the US, on November 25th the first Soviet liquid fuel rocket is launched and reaches the altitude of 80m Fox Films in the US signs Shirley Temple (1928-2014), 5 years and 8 months old,

only 4 years and 3 months older than Corneliu, to a studio contract (less than 4 months later Shirley Temple appears in her first movie, "Stand Up & Cheer") "), and, in Canada, the Dominion of Newfoundland reverts to being a crown colony of Great Britain.
The Chancellor of the University of Oxford is E. F. L. Wood, The Earl of Halifax (1881 – 1959, Chancellor 1933 – 1959, Viceroy of India, Foreign Secretary, and Ambassador to the USA).

Milton's quote: *Give me the liberty to know, to utter, and to argue freely according to conscience, above all liberties.*

424 BC. Little Plato was 4 years old, and his father died. His mother married a second time, to Pyrilampes, a member of the Periclean group.

Demosthenes and Hippocrates attempt to capture Megara, but they are defeated by the Spartans under their general Brasidas. Demosthenes and Hippocrates are unable to coordinate their attacks and Hippocrates is defeated at the Battle of Delium by Pagondas of Thebes. During the battle, Socrates (470 BC – 399 BC) is said to have saved the life of Strategos (General) Alcibiades (450 BC – 404 BC). Demosthenes attacks Sicyon and is defeated as well.

Brasidas' capture of the city of Amphipolis is a major reverse for Athens, for which the Athenian general (and future historian) Thucydides (460 BC – 400 BC) is held responsible and banished. This gives Thucydides the opportunity for undistracted study for his *History of the Peloponnesian War* and for travel and wider contacts, especially on the Peloponnesian side (Sparta and its allies).

Plato's quote: *Necessity is the mother of invention.*

J. R. Lucas on November 3, 2006, at the International Conference "John Stuart Mill, 1806 – 2006".

1934. Little John is 5 years old, and he is much more active, under the permanent care of his mother and father.

On February 9th, 1934, in Athens, Greece, the Pact of Balkan Entente alliance forms between Yugoslavia, Greece, Turkey and Romania, to defend themselves against territorial expansion, but the Soviet Union, Hungary, Bulgaria, Albania and Italy refused to sign the document. A day later Stalin (1878-1953) ends the 17th congress of the Communist Party of the Soviet Union. On March 1st, Henry Pu Yi is crowned emperor Kang Teh of Manchuria, by Japan. Rudolf Kuhnold presents the first radar in Kiel, Germany, on March 20th. Karlis Ulmanis names himself fascist dictator of Latvia on May 15th, 1934. Four days later there is a military coup, by Col Damian Veltsjev, in Bulgaria. On June 9th, the first Donald Duck cartoon, in Wise Little Hen, is released in the US. RCA Victor releases the first 33 1/3 rotations/minute recording, with Ludwig van Beethoven's (1770-1827) Symphony Number 5 in Mi minor (1808). Also the USSR joins the League of Nations, with the Netherlands, Switzerland and Portugal voting no. On October 1st, 1934, Hitler expands German army and navy, and creates an air force, violating the 15 years old Treaty of Versailles (June 28, 1919). On October

16th, Mao Zedong (1893-1976) and 25,000 troops begin the Long March (9000 km over 370 days) to retreat from the attacks of the troops of Chiang Kai-shek (1887-1975). On November 23rd, an Anglo-Ethiopian boundary commission in the Ogaden discovers an Italian garrison at Walwal, which lay well within Ethiopian territory. This leads to the Abyssinia Crisis. On December 29th 1934, Japan renounces the Washington Naval Treaty of 1922 (which limited naval construction) and the London Naval Treaty of 1930 (which regulated submarine warfare and limited naval shipbuilding).

Newton's quote: *Natura valde simplex est et sibi consona* - Nature is exceedingly simple and harmonious with itself.

423 BC. Little Plato is 5.
Darius II becomes king of Persia and Pharaoh of Egypt, 423 BC – 404 BC.

The Athenian general, Laches, convinces the Athenian Assembly to work for an armistice with Sparta. However, the "Truce of Laches" has little impact on Brasidas and collapses within a year.

Brasidas ignores the proposed year-long truce and proceeds to take Scione and Mende in the hope of reaching Athens and freeing Spartan prisoners. Athens sends reinforcements under Nicias who retakes Mende.

Plato's quote: *The worst of all deceptions is self-deception.*

1935. Little John is 6 years old, he was growing fast, and he noticed the General Elections. He liked very much the trains, having a working knowledge of all the local lines, and a strong desire to be an engine-driver when he grew up.

Later Lucas wrote:

"I have always been interested in trains. My mother used to take me along the Portsmouth Road in Guildford to St Catherine's, and then down to the railway bridge, where we would watch the signal and then wait for trains going between the two tunnels and under the bridge. I remember being sad when, on the last day of the steam service to Portsmouth, I saw just South of St Catherine's, a tank engine on almost its last journey pulling a train northwards. (Actually, it was not curtains for the tank engines: they were relegated to the Somerset and Dorset line, where they ousted the more romantic King Arthur class---or so I was later informed by

Beckingham, a knowledgeable boy at my first Prep School, Sunnydown.)

(I was puzzled by electric trains. How did electricity make them go? I concluded that the electrons must come out of the wire and were squirted against the as-it-were-water-wheels of the engine, and thus pushed it round. Later I had an electric motor of my own, powered by a four-and-a-half-volt battery, and could see that this was not the case, but I have never really understood electromagnetism, and still cannot write down Maxwell's equations from memory.)

I played a lot with toy trains. On one occasion I interrupted my father's weekly meeting with the curates to arrange who should do what, and demanded that he should activate a model steam locomotive, which had been given him for my benefit, which he did. There were no rails, and the steam engine careered across the floor of the study, with the curates jumping about to avoid being hit.

My heart was in steam. On one occasion Ginger, who was about ten years old, and was travelling with his fellow train-spotter from Bedford to Cambridge, unburdened himself to me, and said that he would give up engine-spotting when diesels came in, because there was no romance in them. I heartily concurred, and a few years later felt a pang as we travelled on the line to Bournemouth just before it was electrified.

Later, still, I made a point of going to Exeter Central with my son, Edward, aged about five, to see the last steam engine going to Yeovil Town; The engine-driver and fireman lifted Edward up onto the foot-plate, so that he could see into the fire box, and have some sense of what made the wheels go round.

In the wakeful watches of the night I often thought of railway systems.

At one time, soon after retiring, I used to visualise a very tall, walled mediaeval city, but with four railway lines issuing from a high-up opening, and springing out like a flying buttress. The lines did not go anywhere further, and I never saw the point of them, but the image kept on recurring for about a year. Later, I was more concerned with junctions, and would design flyovers to avoid awkward crossings and wrong-way working, as at Didcot; I imagined fly-overs for the Cambridge line on the old Great Eastern and near Rugby on the old London and North Western line."

John was occupied in playing, sometimes with his brother and sisters, often by himself. On his sixth birthday, John was lying outside the house, looking up at the sky, comprehending that he should never be five again, and rather wishing that it were not the case that the past was irrevocable.

The first US surgical operation for relief of angina pectoris was performed in Cleveland, and the inventor Edwin Armstrong gave the first public demonstration of FM broadcasting in the United States, at Alpine, New Jersey.

Prime Minister of the United Kingdom is Stanley Baldwin (1867 – 1947, PM 1935 – 1937, FRS, the only PM to have served under three monarchs (George V, Edward VIII and George VI)).

Newton's quote: *If I have seen further than others, it is by standing upon the shoulders of giants.*

422 BC. Little Plato is 6.

Athenian leader, Cleon, ends the truce between Athens and Sparta. Under Brasidas, the Spartans rout the Athenians in the Battle of Amphipolis. Both Brasidas and Cleon are killed in the battle. Alcibiades takes over the leadership of the pro-war party in Athens. Socrates serves at Battle of Amphipolis.

Aristophanes' (446 BC – 386 BC) play *The Wasps* is performed.

Plato's quote: *The penalty that good men pay for not being interested in politics is to be governed by men worse than themselves.*

1936. Little John is 7 years old, and has started learning Latin from Miss Willan, his governess, and has mastered the Greek alphabet, which encourages his father to take him through the first verses of St John's Gospel. But it was too much for him, and he breaks down in tears. In his old age he returned to the passage, but still has not mastered it.

John goes to St Mary's College.

Edward VIII (1894 – 1972) succeeds, on January 20, 1936, British king George V (1865 – 1936), but King Edward VIII marries Mrs. Wallis Simpson, and abdicates throne after 10 months and 22 days, on December 11, 1936. The Duke of York becomes, on December 11, 1936, King George VI (1895 – 1952). The President of the British Academy is Sir David Ross (1877 – 1971, President 1936 – 1940, Scottish philosopher with works in ethics), Italian troops occupy Addis Ababa, the capital city of Ethiopia. The 11th Olympic Games take place in Berlin, August 1 – 16, 1936. Germany and Japan sign the anti-Komintern pact. After many Japanese attacks, the Chinese leader Chiang Kai-shek declares war on Japan.

Newton's quote: *I do not know what I may appear to the world; but to myself I seem to have been only like a boy playing on the seashore, and diverting myself now and then finding a smoother pebble or a prettier shell than ordinary, whilst the great ocean of truth lay all undiscovered before me.*

421 BC. Little Plato is 7, and he received a musical and gymnastic education; he wrote juvenile epigrams and tragedies, but burned them once he became associated with Socrates.

Nicias, the leader of the aristocratic and peace party in Athens, and Pleistoanax, King of Sparta, negotiate the Peace of Nicias between Athens and Sparta, which brings a temporary end to the Peloponnesian War. All of Sparta's allies agree to sign the peace, except for the Boeotians, Corinth, Elis, and Megara.

The city of Cumae, the most northerly of the Greek colonies in Italy, falls to the Samnites.

The construction of the *Porch of the Maidens* (the Caryatid Porch) commences at the Erechtheion, which is part of the Acropolis in Athens.

Plato's quote: *Any man may easily do harm, but not every man can do good to another.*

1937. John is 8 years old, and much later, he writes:

"Uncle Reggie once told me that I was bumptious, as we walked along a lane (see below) in 1937 or 1938. He could equally have called me conceited, being very much aware of the limited knowledge of most of those around me.

Uncle Reggie used to walk along the lanes swinging his stick to knock off the growing fronds of brambles. It was important to get exactly the right spot; if the stick hit the woody part, the woody part would swing under the blow and swing back; so too if blow landed nearer the end of the growing frond, which would likewise swing under the blow and then swing back. Only if there was no room for the frond to swing and the woody stem resisted the blow, would the frond be knocked off."

The first Charlie Chaplin talkie, "Modern Times," is released in the US. The first US congressional session takes place in air-conditioned chambers. Japanese troops conquer Nanjing (China),
Prime Minister of the United Kingdom is Neville Chamberlain (1869 – 1940, PM 1937 – 1940, FRS, and he signed the Munich Agreement; he died six months after leaving office).
Newton's quote: *Men build too many walls and not enough bridges.*

420 BC. Little Plato is 8.
The young and popular Alcibiades is elected "Strategos" (one of a board of ten generals) and begins to dominate Athenian life and politics. A Quadruple Alliance of Athens, Argos, Mantineia and Elis, which has been organized by Alcibiades (in opposition to Nicias), confronts a Spartan-Boeotian alliance.
Euripides' (480 BC – 406 BC) play *The Suppliant Women* is performed.
Protagoras, Greek pre-Socratic philosopher (b. c. 490 BC), passes away at 70.
Plato's quote: *Every heart sings a song, incomplete, until another heart whispers back.*

1938. Little John is 9 years old, and much later he writes:
"I had two operations earlier in 1938 on my ears. The first was a small one, done in Mummy's and Daddy's bedroom to make a small hole in my eardrum to let the pus out. I was anaesthetized with ethyl chloride. The doctor made a joke of its being a girl's name. (I had been sleeping on a low bed there for some time while I was ill. I remember being sick once on the carpet, which later was in their bedroom in Durham.) The operation did not clear my ear,

and I had another, full dress one in hospital, where I was anaesthetized with chloroform administered through an orange mask and an orange flexible wrinkly tube about 1 1/2 inches in diameter. I was told to count out loud. I had a deep intuition of atheism and something wrinkly closing in upon me. I stopped counting, and then thought I should be hurt, and desperately shouted out another number or two before losing consciousness.

I remember the day in September 1938 when I was due to go to the Dragon School. I was in the lower garden of St Nicolas Rectory, at the South end of the tennis court, under the apple tree, wearing a blue suit. The news came that tests had shown that I was not well enough to go. I was very glad. During the autumn I had two operations, one to scorch my tonsils, the other, more serious one, to take them out. I little thought how upset my father must have been at the waste of a whole term's fees, and the diminishing prospects of my winning a scholarship to go to Winchester. Also, I now wonder, whether if I had gone to the Dragon in September instead of January, I might have been befriended by ``The Skipper; who had a genius for understanding unhappy small boys, and been reconciled to a Draconian existence.

In 1938, when I was at Sunnydown, the Headmaster announced at Morning assembly the momentous news that Germany had occupied the Sudetenland."

German troops invade Austria (Anschluss); instant coffee is invented in the US; archaeologists discover engraved gold and silver plates from King Darius (550 BC – 486 BC) in Persepolis (Iran); the Treaty of Munich is signed by Hitler, Mussolini, Daladier (1884 – 1970) and Chamberlain (1869 – 1940); Germany annexes Sudetenland (1/3 of Czechoslovakia); Japanese troops occupy Canton, Hankou and Wuhan in China; DuPont, in the US, announces its new synthetic fiber will be called "nylon"; a fascist coup in Romania fails; a French-German non-attack treaty is signed (Ribbentrop-Bonnet Pact).

Newton's quote: *Tact is the art of making a point without making an enemy.*

419 BC. Little Plato is 9.

The Peace of Nicias is still being in effect, but Sparta's King Agis II gathers a strong army at Philus and descends upon Argos. He is able to conclude a treaty with Argos.

Euripides' play *Andromache* is performed.

Sophocles' (497 BC – 406 BC) play *Electra* is performed.

Sophocles' quote: *To be doing good deeds is man's most glorious task.*

Chapter 2: Lucas at Durham

In 1939 the Lucas family moved from Guildford to Durham on the appointment of the Reverend E. de G. Lucas to be Archdeacon of Durham.

Twenty years earlier the Reverend A.P.T. Williams, planned to spend it as a curate at Rudmore under him, when he, then a don at Winchester, had been going to have a term's sabbatical leave. But it came to nothing. Further commitments at Winchester precluded his being able to be absent in Portsmouth. He became successively Second Master and Head Master of Winchester, Dean of Christ Church, and was about to become Bishop of Durham. The might-have-been curate chose his would-have-been vicar to be his deputy in running his diocese.

Paul Lucas, John's brother, tells of their mother being in tears as they drove into the far-off North, away from all her friends and acquaintances. But in fact the close-knit community around the Cathedral at Durham gave her close friends, and turned out to be the happiest years of her life, as well as being a formative influence on the lives of her children. Although County Durham was dominated by coal-mining, steel-making and ship-building, the City of Durham, and particularly the Cathedral and Castle, situated on a peninsula surrounded by the river Wear, constituted a fortress of resistance and dominance: of resistance to the marauding Scots in the Middle Ages and to the rumbling discontent of the laboring classes in the Twentieth Century, and the supremacy of order and civilization over everyone.

Many years later Lucas writes:
"In many different ways the Cathedral shaped my aspirations and enlarged my understanding.
On one Sunday we had hymn 423 in the English Hymnal, Judge Eternal, throned in splendor. The last couplet of v. 2:
``And the homesteads and the woodlands

plead in silence for their peace."
moved me to tears. I had already become, and have remained throughout all my life, extremely sensitive to natural beauty, especially that of the English countryside.

On another occasion, the last Sunday of the Easter holidays, 1942, we had psalm 126. The verses:
"They that sow in tears shall reap in joy He that goeth on his way weeping, and beareth forth good seed, shall doubtless come in joy and bring his sheaves with him."
spoke to me. I was about to go back to the Dragon School, and try for a scholarship to Winchester, which, if I got it, would mean I should come back in joy, and never have to go to that school again.

Much later, when I was an undergraduate, I had been learning that the axioms of geometry were purely formal, and could be interpreted in all sorts of ways. But I saw the shafts of sunlight coming through the clerestory windows, and showing straight edges in the smoky (or dusty) atmosphere.

They were evidently straight, and not because they happened to satisfy some axioms of incidence in a geometry. So straightness was not defined by geometrical axioms but had an independent meaning. The austerely formal approach to geometry did not tell the whole truth.

In Durham I had to abandon my previous view that grown-ups were mostly stupid and ill informed. Durham was full of knowledgeable and highly intelligent men. Professor Wager was an atheist, but quite ready to talk geology with me. Professor Wagstaff once had me in his laboratory, and did an experiment that made me understand angular momentum.

The ecclesiastics had the edge on the other academics. The Dean, Cyril Argentine Alington, had indeed a silver tongue and a wonderful way with words. On one occasion my father was sent a missive: ``Read Mark, 10:18 and tell the people truth, not lies", which he showed to him, and shortly afterwards received the response: Such terrifying beacons are very rightly seen as guidance by Archdeacons, But don't concern a Dean.

Having been a headmaster, Dean Alington was inclined to be autocratic, but encountered effective resistance from the Chapter. When he wanted to install yet another window designed by Easton, Canon Ramsey intoned the verse from Clough's hymn, ``Not by Eastern Windows only, . . . ''. On another occasion, Canon Richardson did not occupy exactly the place the Dean had specified. After the service the Dean said angrily ``If you had done that at school, you'd have been fired'', to which Canon Richardson retorted, ``Yes. That's what cannons are for''.

The Bishop lacked the Dean's facility with language, but had a much deeper and more powerful mind, and was later on the panel which produced the Revised Version of the King James Bible. When Canon Quick left to become Regius Professor of Divinity at Oxford, he was succeeded by Canon Ramsey, who after leaving to become Regius Professor of Divinity at Cambridge, returned to be Bishop of Durham, and ended up as Archbishop of Canterbury.

I was growing up in a society of immensely able and dedicated men, who were invariably ready to find time to talk to me, and encourage me to think for myself. I contrast its norms with those encountered by my grand-daughter today. Recently her teacher confided in her how unhappy she was at the breaking up of her relationship with her lover. Divorce, adultery, betrayal, bereavement, rejection and isolation are the common stuff of contemporary existence. In Durham I knew of only one woman who committed suicide when she was discovered having committed adultery while her husband was away on war service. Scandal existed, but was exceptional.

We left Durham in 1952, but Durham did not leave me. I returned in body several times while I was at Leeds, and again when I was giving a lecture on C.S. Lewis and again when Helen graduated, and yet again for another graduation ceremony: and in my mind I still constantly return, and remain in spirit a Durham man forever.'' ,

1939. John, at 9 years and 7 months, goes in January to Dragon School (a preparatory boarding school in Oxford, founded in 1877). The family moved to Durham (a historic city in North East England, on River Wear, 350 km northwest of London, and 200 km southeast of Glasgow). The family lived in The College (i.e. the Close) Durham, until the father retired in 1953. He was one of the very few who was allowed to go with his car on Prebends Bridge (a stone-arch bridge in the center of Durham, opened in 1778) to cross the river Wear. There was a continuous gradient from both the Archdeaconry and from his garage, and occasionally, when he had difficulty in starting his 12 years old car, the car would be pushed to start rolling downhill with the gears in third, and the clutch being let out and in to turn the engine. It always worked, and the Archdeacon was glad, because it would have been shaming to have his car rescued from there.

In June 1939 young Lucas is visited by his parents at the Dragon School, and he is given a "Contour Book for Cyclists, the Eastern Region" and he read of a ride in Northamptonshire, through undulating country. He asked what `dulate' meant, thinking that it must be the opposite of `undulate'. His father explained that `undulate; came from the Latin unda, and young Lucas thought he would like to go to Northamptonshire to see the pleasant undulating countryside.

Much later Lucas writes: "On September 3rd, 1939 I was at Matins in Durham Cathedral, and a messenger came in with a piece of paper, which the Dean then read out, saying that a state of war existed between us and Germany. We spent the next few days filling sand-bags under the guidance of Patrick Alington, the Dean's younger son, who had intended to take Holy Orders, but was killed on Long-stop Hill in Tunisia.

We were fully aware of the seriousness of the situation. Sometime earlier my Uncle Cecil had told my father that Britain did not possess enough shells to fight a single naval battle. In the event we survived by the skin of our teeth. But nobody---and certainly not I---was in doubt about how dire out situation was."

The uranium atom first split takes place at Columbia University, USA; Eugenio Pacelli was chosen as Pope Pius XII

(1876 – 1958); Germany occupies Czechoslovakia; Hungary annexes the republic of Karpato-Ukraine; the Sino-Japanese War (1937-1945) continues with the Battle of Nanchang; the Spanish Civil War ends and Madrid falls to Francisco Franco (1892 – 1975); Faisal II (1935 – 1958) ascends to the throne of Iraq at the age of 4, and is the last King of Iraq; Italy invades Albania; Hungary leaves the League of Nations; Stalin requests and then signs British-French-Soviet Union anti-nazi pact; Germany and Italy announce an alliance known as the Rome-Berlin Axis; the first king and queen of the UK to visit the USA, George VI and Elizabeth; the test flight of the first rocket plane, using liquid propellants, takes place in Germany; the Russian offensive, under General Zhukov, against Japanese invasion in Mongolia, takes place; Molotov-Ribbentrop pact: East Europe will be divided between Hitler and Stalin - Poland will be divided in half, Bessarabia from Romania will be occupied by Stalin; formally Germany and USSR sign a 10-year non-aggression pact; Belgium, Netherland and Poland mobilize; Isoroku Yamamoto is appointed the supreme commander of the Japanese fleet; the Japanese invasion army is driven out of Mongolia by the Russians; Switzerland proclaims neutrality.

The World War II (WW II) starts, Germany invades Poland, and takes Danzig • Britain declares war on Germany • France follows 6 hours later, quickly joined by Australia, New Zeeland, South Africa and Canada • Netherlands and Belgium declare neutrality • the USA declare themselves neutral • Iraq and Saudi Arabia declare war on Germany • Poland's president Moscicki and Prime Minister Slawoj-Skladkowski flee to Romania • Soviet Union invades Eastern Poland and takes 217,000 prisoners • the Versailles Peace Treaty (June 28, 1919) forgot to include Andorra, so Andorra and Germany finally, after 20 years, sign an official treaty ending World War I • Estonia accepts Soviet military bases • the Soviet-German treaty agrees on the 4th partition of Poland and gives Lithuania to the USSR • last Polish troops surrender and Germany annexes Western Poland • Albert Einstein (1879 – 1955) informs the US President Roosevelt of the possibilities of an atomic bomb • four soviet soldiers are killed on the Finnish-Russian border, then the Soviet government revokes the Russian-Finnish non-attack treaty, and USSR invades Finland and bombs Helsinki • the League of Nations excludes the Soviet Union

Churchill's quote: *It's not enough that we do our best; sometimes we have to do what's required.*

418 BC. Plato is 10 years old.

The Battle of Mantinea (a city 120 km southwest of Athens) is the largest land battle of the Peloponnesian War (431 BC – 404 BC, with almost 10,000 troops on each side). Sparta, under King Agis II, has a major victory over Argos (30 km east of Mantinea, and its allies Athens, Ellis and Mantinea). The commander of the Athenian forces, Laches, is killed in the battle. Socrates (52) fights in the Battle of Mantinea as a hoplite (armored soldier).

Argos changes its government from democracy to aristocracy, and ends its support for Athens in favor of an alliance with Sparta. Many of Argos' allies do the same. Athens becomes increasingly isolated.

Alcibiades (450 BC – 404 BC) urges the Athenians to conquer Syracuse (southeast of Sicily), subdue Sicily and Carthage (seaside suburb of Tunisia's capital Tunis, 200 km southwest of Sicily). He wins the support of the Athenians.

Plato's quote: *How can you prove whether at this moment we are sleeping, and all our thoughts are a dream; or whether we are awake, and talking to one another in the waking state?*

1940. John is 11 years old goes to school, and feels the great concerns of his parents.

John's cousin Priscilla Dobbs is born.

President of the British Academy is Sir J. H. Clapham (1873 – 1946, President 1940-1946, Professor of Economic History at Cambridge University).

Let's see some of the events in 1940: Sergei Prokofiev's (1891 – 1953) ballet Romeo and Juliet premieres in Leningrad • Soviets bomb cities in Finland • the Polish pianist and composer Ignace Jan Paderewski (1860 – 1941), Knight Grand Cross of the Order of the British Empire, at 80 becomes premier of the Polish government in exile   the first opera telecast, in New York City, is "I Pagliacci" (written in 1892) by Ruggero Leoncavallo (1857 – 1919) • Finland surrenders to the USSR and gives Karelische Isthmus • Mussolini joins Hitler in Germany's war against France and Britain • Karelo-Finnish SSR becomes the 12th Soviet republic (until 1956) • Germany invades Norway and Denmark (Denmark surrenders) • Italy annexes Albania • British troops land at Narvik, Norway • the first electron microscope is presented by RCA in Philadelphia, USA • Rear Admiral Joseph Taussig testifies, before the US Senate Naval Affairs Committee, that war with Japan is inevitable   Norwegian King Haakon VII (1872 – 1957, King for 52 years) and his government flee to England • the 1940 Olympics at Helsinki are cancelled • Winston Churchill (1874 – 1965) succeeds Neville Chamberlain as Prime Minister of United Kingdom (1940 – 1945) • German armies attack The Netherlands, Belgium and Luxembourg • Germany blitz conquest of France begins by crossing Meuse River • Dutch Queen Wilhelmina (1880 – 1962, Queen for nearly 58 years, starting at age 10) flees to England • Germany bombs Rotterdam, The Netherlands, (600 dead) • The Netherlands surrender to Germany • McDonald's opens its first restaurant in San Bernardino, California • Germany occupies Brussels, Belgium • French tanks counter attack at Pronne, under General Charles de Gaulle (1890 – 1970) • the first successful helicopter flight takes place in the US, with Vought-Sikorsky US-300, designed by the Russian American aviation pioneer Igor Ivanovich Sikorsky (1889 – 1972, immigrated to the US in 1919) • Operation Dynamo begins, to evacuate defeated Allied troops from Dunkirk, France • Belgium surrenders to Germany and King Leopold III (1901 – 1983) gives himself up • British-French troops capture Narvik in Norway • Premier Winston Churchill flies to Paris to meet with the 84 years old Marshal Philippe Pétain (1856 – 1951) , who announced he is willing to make a separate peace with Germany • German forces enter Paris • British and French troops evacuate Narvik in Norway • the discovery of the first chemical transuranic element with atomic number 93, neptunium (Np, a radioactive actinide metal, named after planet Neptune, itself named after Roman god of the sea Neptune), is announced in the US • General Charles de Gaulle's first meeting with Winston Churchill • Norway surrenders to Germany • Italy declares war on allies and raids Malta • in response, British forces bomb Genoa and Torino in Italy • France surrenders to Germany and German troops occupy Paris • Soviet Army occupies Lithuania and installs a communist government, then occupies Estonia • General Charles de Gaulle on BBC tells

French people to defy the German occupiers • France signs an armistice with Italy • USSR ends the use of an experimental calendar, and returns to Gregorian calendar • Soviet Army attacks Romania and Romania cedes Bessarabia to the Soviet Union • Hitler orders invasion of England (Operation Sealion) • British Royal Navy sinks the French fleet in North Africa • the diplomatic relations are broken between Britain and Vichy government in France • Battle of Britain begins as German forces attack by air for 114 days • Soviet Union annexes Estonia, Latvia and Lithuania • Italian troops invade British Somalia (in the Horn of Africa, near the Gulf of Aden) • Churchill recognizes De Gaulle French government in exile • Alsace Lorraine from France is annexed by the Third Reich (name for Germany from 1933 to 1945) • Greece mobilizes • General George Marshall is sworn in as chief of staff of the US army • the first showing of the high definition color TV takes place in the USA • Crown prince (19 years old) Mihai (Michael, born 1921) succeeds Carol II as king of Romania • 4 teens, going down a hole near Lascaux, France, discover 17,000-year-old drawings, now known as the Lascaux Cave Paintings • Japanese troops attack French Indo-China • Germany, Italy and Japan sign a 10 year formal alliance (Axis) • German troops occupy Romania • 40 hour work week goes into effect in the USA • Italy attacks Greece, but Greece successfully resists • Hungary, Romania and Slovakia join the Axis Powers • • British troops have their first major offensive in North Africa • Germany begins dropping incendiary bombs on London.

Churchill's quote: *Never in the field of human conflict was so much owed by so many to so few.*

417 BC. Plato is 11 years old.

Because of the loss by Athens in the Battle of Mantinea, a political struggle takes place in Athens. Alcibiades joins forces with Nicias (470 BC - 413 BC) against Hyperbolus (circa 460 BC – 411 BC), the successor of the demagogue politician Cleon. Nicias and Alcibiades combine their influence to convince the Athenian people to expel Hyperbolus.

Plato's quote: *The human behavior flows from three main sources: desire, emotion, and knowledge.*

J. R. Lucas on November 3, 2006, at the International Conference "John Stuart Mill, 1806 – 2006".

1941. John 12 years old continues at the Dragon School. His parents concerned not for his safety but for his progress: will he be able to get a scholarship? Mr. Higmeister, the Senior Mathematics Master tells them that he is sure that he will win one, though he is not confident that he will manage on his maths alone.

Canada and US acquire air bases in Newfoundland (99 years lease) • Kuomintang forces under orders from Chiang Kai-Shek open fire at communist forces, resuming the Chinese Civil War • British offensive in Eritrea takes place • British and Australian troops capture Tobruk, North Africa, from Italians • British troops march into Abyssinia (Ethiopian Empire) • Japanese armored barges cross Strait of Johore to attack Singapore • plutonium is first produced and isolated by the American chemist, with Nobel Prize in Chemistry, Dr. Glenn T. Seaborg (1912 – 1999) • German troops invade Bulgaria, then Bulgaria joined the Axis Pact • 50,000 British soldiers land in Greece • Britain leases defense bases in Trinidad (near Venezuela) to US for 99 years • Churchill warns Stalin of a plan for a German invasion of the USSR • the operation Bestrafung begins - Germany bombers attack Belgrade, Yugoslavia, 17,000 die Italian held Addis Ababa (Ethiopia) surrenders to British and Ethiopian forces • pact of neutrality between the USSR and

Japan is signed • the Kingdom of Yugoslavia surrenders to Germany • Bulgarian troops invade Macedonia in Greece • 100 German bombers attack Athens, Greece • Greece surrenders to Germany • Operation Merkur: Hitler orders the conquest of Crete (the largest Greek island, in the south) • Stalin becomes premier of USSR • Konrad Zuse presents the Z3, the world's first working programmable, fully automatic computer, in Berlin • the first British turbojet flies • Italian army under General Aosta surrenders to Britain at Amba Alagi, Ethiopia • Germany invades Crete, Greece • British troops attack Baghdad, Iraq • the USA declares state of emergency, due to Germany's sinking of the US ship Robin Moor • a German Luftwaffe air raid on Dublin, Ireland, claims 38 lives • Germany bans all Catholic publications • English and French troops overthrow the pro-German Syrian government Estonians start armed resistance against the Soviet occupation • Finland invades Karelia • Operation Barbarossa: Germany attacks the Soviet Union and occupies the Baltic states • Germany, Italy, Romania and Finland declare war on the Soviet Union • US forces land in Iceland to forestall Germany invasion • Beirut, Lebanon, is occupied by Free France and British troops • the pharmaceutical-grade penicillin is produced in large quantities by Pfizer in Brooklyn, New York, USA • British Prime Minister Winston Churchill launched his "V for Victory" campaign • the USA demand Japanese troops out of Indo-China and start embargo on oil-export to Japan • The US President Franklin Roosevelt and British Prime Minister Winston Churchill issue the joint declaration that later becomes known as the Atlantic Charter • German troops reach Leningrad • English and Russian troops attack pro-German Iran and Reza Shah Pahlavi (1878 – 1944) of Iran is forced to abdicate throne to his son Mohammad Reza Pahlavi (1919 – 1980) • the blockade of Leningrad (St. Petersburg) by Germany begins • Roosevelt orders any Axis ships found in American waters to be shot on sight • the U.S. Navy is ordered to attack German U-boats • the construction of the Pentagon for the US Department of Defense begins (completed on January 15, 1943) • General de Gaulle forms the French government in exile in London • nine Allied governments pledge adherence to the common principles of the policy set forth in the Atlantic Charter • German troops start an assault on Moscow: operation Taifun begins • USA lends Soviet

Union $1 million • Germany's drive to take Moscow is halted • Mussolini's forces leave Abyssinia (Ethiopia) • Japanese emperor Hirohito (1901 – 1989) secretly signs declaration of war against the USA on December 1st, 1941 • German siege of Tobruk (port in Libya, near Egypt), after 8 months, ends • Japanese attack Pearl Harbor, Hawaii, USA, on December 7, 1941 • in London, the Dutch government in exile declares war on Japan and Italy • the US and Britain declare war on Japan, and the USA enters the World War II • China declares war on Germany and Italy Germany and Italy declare war on the USA • Dutch and Australian troops land on the island Portuguese Timor (south of Indonesia, 500 km north of Australia) • German troops led by the field marshal Erwin Rommel (1891 – 1944) begin retreating in North Africa • Japanese troops land on Hong Kong • Hitler takes complete command of the German Army • Premier Winston Churchill arrives in Washington, DC, for a wartime conference • Japan announces the surrender of the British-Canadian garrison in Hong Kong • Winston Churchill becomes the first British Prime Minister to address a joint meeting of the Congress of the USA, warning that the Axis would "stop at nothing" • Japan bombs Manila, capital of Philippines, even though it was declared an "open city" • Winston Churchill addresses the Canadian parliament.

Churchill's quote: *Never, never, never give up.*

416 BC. Plato is 12 years old.
Birth of Socrates' son Lamprokles.
The Athenians take the island of Melos (volcanic island in the Aegean Sea, north of the Sea of Crete, the southwestern most island in the Cyclades group, 150 km southeast of Athens, famous for the statue of Aphrodite (the *"Venus de Milo"*, now in the Louvre), and also for statues of the Greek god Asclepius (now in the British Museum), which has remained neutral during the Peloponnesian War). Its inhabitants are treated with great cruelty by the Athenians, which increases the hostility against the Athenians.
In Sicily, the Ionian city of Segesta (west of Sicily, 50 km southwest of Palermo) asks for Athenian help against the Dorian city of Selinus (40 km south of Segesta). Selinus is supported by the powerful Sicilian city of Syracuse (250 km southeast of Selinus). The people of Syracuse are ethnically Dorian (as are the Spartans),

while the Athenians, and their allies in Sicily, are Ionian. The Athenians prepare an armada to attack Sicily.

Plato's quote: *I exhort you also to take part in the great combat, which is the combat of life, and greater than every other earthly conflict.*

J. R. Lucas on November 3, 2006, at the International Conference "John Stuart Mill, 1806 – 2006".

Chapter 3: Lucas at Winchester

On June 6th, 1942, John Lucas was congratulated by John G. Winant, the American Ambassador to Britain, on winning a scholarship to Winchester. Mr. Winant was visiting Durham, and was welcomed at the North Door of the Cathedral, by the Bishop and the Dean and Chapter, among them Lucas's father, who had shortly before been rung up by an ecstatic son to say he had won a scholarship. His father could not contain himself, but had to tell the good news to the Bishop, who had been Head Master of Winchester, whereupon Mr. Winant added his congratulations.

Winchester had always been in his sights---he remembered Gunners' Hole, the school bathing place, being pointed out to him on the way to Southampton---for at his christening his two Godfathers (his Uncle Cecil and Monty Rendall) agreed they must see to it that he went to the best Prep school and the best Public school. And Winchester might have been possible, even without the scholarship. Many years later Lucas remembered being told by his father that on some occasion in the 1930s the then Head Master, Spencer Leeson, had told him that Winchester had reached an agreement with Marlborough that the schoolmasters at each could send their sons to the other at a greatly reduced rate. My father said it sounded a very good scheme, but it would be even better if Winchester College Missioners were included too. Spencer Leeson agreed and said that it should be so.

Nevertheless, winning a scholarship was important, and not easy. Lucas remembers little of the exam. One question in the General Paper was on music, to describe briefly a concerto, a sonata, a symphony etc., which he could do quickly, but then went on to ask for a description of one's favourite bit of music. He described ``Brother James' Air". Afterwards his form master, on asking what he had done, thought it a great mistake, and that the examiners would have expected a critical account of a Bach concerto or Beethoven symphony; but actually it may have served him well, giving the impression that he was genuinely making his own view, and not regurgitating accepted opinions, and clearly not the result of careful schooling.

June 6th, 1942, was indeed a pivotal point in Lucas's life. On the material side the bounty of William of Wykeham not only paid for five years at Winchester, but provided him with further support for his undergraduate years at Oxford. More importantly, he was always among others who were in various respects cleverer than he was himself, so that he always had to struggle to keep up. He could not rest on his laurels or suppose that he could drift to the top. Only hard work would do.

It was not feasible in war time for Lucas to be brought from Durham to Winchester for his formal admission to College. So he came a day early, and stayed overnight with his Aunt and Godmother, who was married to the Vicar of King's Sombourne, about ten miles West of Winchester. The next afternoon he was directed to his bed in Twelfth Chamber, where he found Mark Morford, who was to become a life-long friend, being dressed in scholar's uniform by his mother. The uniform consisted of a black cloth gown over a curiously shaped waist-coat, and pinstripe trousers. Lucas thought that the blue trousers he was wearing would, saving the trouble of taking them off and putting the pinstripe ones on, but Mrs. Morford decreed otherwise, and a sartorial misdemeanor was averted. The scholars were admitted one by one in Roll order, each one kneeling before the Warden, who started with an admonition that each should think of what he could give rather than what he could get.

Lucas, many years later, records:
That night, when I was in bed, Christopher Brook came round to Twelfth, where Mark Morford and I were the new men, to pay a call on our two-year men, Tony Cockshut and ``Megalo" Cole. In one of the Chamber Annals it was reported that Christopher Brook ``could argue the hind leg off a mediaeval donkey". (I had some conversation with him when we were received Ad Portas, and we occasionally met when I visited Cambridge. He collaborated with a Merton colleague of mine, J.R.L. Highfield in producing a---largely picture---book of Oxford and Cambridge.) Later on

Cockshut and Cole talked about Roger Toulmin who was also a two-year man. They foresaw him going to the bad, and ending up as a monk in South America. I was immensely impressed, and thought I had entered the real world, where people went to the bad, and ended up as monks in South America.

My first year at Winchester was difficult.
I had been given extra marks at Election on account of being young, but actually was weaker than my contemporaries, and had to struggle to keep up. I was barely managing to do so, but then had a stroke of good fortune: we did the Prayer Book; one of the questions was what bit occurred in only one of the services of Morning and Evening Prayer. Almost everyone put down the anthem, which in Chapel only came at Evensong, but I knew it was the Venite, thus scoring full marks, and catching up with the others.

At the end of my first year I opted for the science ladder. The Headmaster thought I should stay on the classics ladder, but I was very keen on chemistry. (He, however, might reckon he was vindicated, when I spent most of my working life as a member of the Oxford Literae Humaniores faculty). I was taught by Harold Walker, who was a marvellous teacher. I have been greatly advantaged by having a good grounding in the history of the Ancient World, the early Middle Ages and the United States. When doing the War of Independence, he told us that the rebels' cause was best argued for in Britain, and the best case for staying in the Empire was articulated by Americans---a point not widely known, but of great importance for an understanding of American history, and sometimes applicable to other conflicts. On several occasions, when arguing with Americans, I have been able to confound them by citing facts and precepts from their own history that they were unaware of.

The following year we were under the guidance of Eric James. Eric James was inspirational. Under him Hugh Storey, Martin Beale and I jockeyed for first place, each of us succeeding once, I in the final summer term. I now wonder whether Eric favoured me unduly. My ``original task", a home-made cannon working with a spring mounted on two carpet wheels, was not as original as Martin's, a musical composition. In any case, I had let Eric down badly, because on one occasion I had cheated. He had set a piece of prose with the adjectives left out, and we were to put in ones we thought were appropriate. I saw that he was reading from the Oxford Book of English Prose, and to my shame looked up the piece of Conrad ``And this is how I see the East'', and made up suitable alternatives to the actual adjectives used. It was not in the critical Cloister time, which secured my place at the top of the Science Ladder thereafter; but I remain ashamed.

Again I was very well served by my teachers: I owe a great deal to John Manisty.
I was so well taught that though not having specialised in mathematics I was able to switch from chemistry to mathematics when I went up to Oxford. I remember in particular his explaining differential coefficients in terms of a dialogue: you say how close to the tangent you want the chord to be, and I will find the coordinates of a chord that will satisfy your requirement. This made it easy to understand the epsilon-delta definitions and arguments when I came across them in Oxford, and similarly the interplay of universal and existential quantifiers in symbolic logic. I have made great use of it in my philosophical thought. It underlies my first published article in Philosophy, 1955.

I remember being asked out to tea, together with someone else by John Manisty and Ronald Hamilton, and having tea in a first-floor room in College Street. I have a vague impression of his being very welcoming and friendly, but the details elude me.

From GCHQ Material in The National Archives sent to Edward on 22/11/11 by Tony Comer Departmental Historian

John Manisty came to Bletchley Park as a mathematician from Marlborough College. He spent most of the war in Hut 6 (German Army and Air Force cryptanalysis). In mid-1942 he was one of Hut 6's Bombe Controllers, responsible for sharing out Bombe processing capability between Huts 6 and 8. He has the reputation of being very concerned with the security of the output of Enigma processing: the only document which is identified as by him in The National Archives is in piece reference HW 14/90: "Capt JC

Manisty to PS Milner-Barry on subject of Enigma clearance or people 'in the know' October 16 1943, requests list of cleared personnel, passed on by Milner-Barry to AD (S), reply from AD (S) Oct 28." Manisty replaced Milner-Barry as Head of what was left of Hut 6 in July 1945, but left soon after to go into the teaching profession.

Most of the wartime histories have been released but are almost all written in the passive and without naming names, so it would be difficult to pick out what he did.

He is mentioned in "Code Breakers", edited by Hinsley and Stripp in an article by Derek Taunt, who worked with him in Hut 6:

"Mention of Christmas reminds me of the incomparable John Manisty. Every community needs a railway timetable wizard, and JC was one par excellence. He also controlled the shift and leave rotas, and knew to a tee the preferences and alliances of the staff. You could save up your weekly day off until you had two or three days in hand, and could make the most of them by taking them after a night shift and returning on an evening shift. John managed such arrangements with tact and finesse and certainly helped us to survive the traumas of wartime travel by rail."

Harold Walker's course on the Ancient World was an effective corrective to the Classicists' assumption, easily gleaned from Latin and Greek sources, that the Orientals were all barbarians. In fact the civilisations of the East were highly developed, with great skills, craftsmanship and literature. The Proverbial Wisdom of the Semitic and Babylonian societies enshrined true insights about the human condition. What the Greeks gave us was the ability to question the received tradition searchingly and constructively. They went beyond. The Greeks created creativity.

Some details about Winchester: Collegium Sanctae Mariae prope Wintoniam, established 1382, motto: Manners makyth man, independent boarding school for boys, located in Winchester (Hampshire, South East of England, 98 km south-west of London and 22 km north from Southampton), considered to have the finest tradition of scholarship, and being uniquely civilized.

Lucas left Winchester in 1947, but retained many links with Winchester, notably in 1953, when he found himself tutoring his erstwhile schoolmates, and in 2011 when along with other Fellows of the British Academy and Fellows of the Royal Society, he was received Ad Portas, thus rounding off his connection with Winchester in the most complete and satisfying way.

Ad Portas in 2011

1942. John is 16 days before his 13th birthday, on June 2nd, when he is elected a scholar of Winchester College.

John's cousin Evelyn Dobbs is born.

In the meantime, there are many big events taking place in this year: the USA, UK and 24 other countries sign a united declaration against the Axis • 28 nations, at war with the Axis, pledge no separate peace • German troops in Bardia, a seaport in Libya near Egypt, surrender • Japanese troops occupy Manila, Philippines • the first US forces in Europe during WW II go ashore in Northern Ireland • Hitler's Operation Sealion (invasion of England) is cancelled • about 150 Japanese warplanes attack the north Australian city of Darwin • the US President Roosevelt orders detention and internment of all west-coast Japanese-Americans • the US President Franklin Roosevelt orders General Douglas MacArthur (1880 – 1964) out of the Philippines, as American defenses collapse • one Japanese submarine fires on an oil refinery in Ellwood, 50 km west of Los Angeles, California, USA • the English physicist and radio astronomer James Stanley Hey (1909 – 2000), Fellow of the Royal Society, discovers radio emissions from the Sun • Roosevelt orders men between 45 and 64 to register for non-military duty • the British Arctic convoy PQ13, with war supplies on 19 British, American and Polish ships, departs Reykjavik, Iceland, to Murmansk, USSR, where only 15 ships arrived (during the war about 1400 ships delivered essential war supplies to the USSR) • The US move native-born of Japanese ancestry into detention centers • Tokyo is bombed by American airplanes • the Battle of the Coral Sea (off the northeast coast of Australia) ends, stopping Japanese expansion • a helicopter makes its first cross-country flight in the USA • Mexico declares war on Germany and Japan • Anglo-Soviet Treaty is signed in London • Battle of Midway (territory of the US, an atoll in the North Pacific Ocean, equidistant between North America and Asia, about one-third of the way from Honolulu, Hawaii to Tokyo, Japan) begins, and this is Japan's first major defeat in WW II, just six months after Japan's attack on Pearl Harbor, Hawaii • USA declares war on Bulgaria, Hungary and Romania • Japanese troops land on the islands Kiska and Attu (2500 km northeast of Japan and 2000 km southwest of continental Alaska), Aleutian Islands, Alaska, USA • German troops march into Sevastopol, a port on the Black Sea, in the southwestern region of the Crimean Peninsula, USSR • the German army is defeated by the British army at El-Alamein, port in Egypt, on the Mediterranean Sea, 106 km west of Alexandria • the US and USSR sign the Lend-Lease agreement during WW II, which gives to the USSR much needed war military assistance from the US • the first V-2 rocket is launched at Peenemunde Army Research Center (Heeresversuchsanstalt Peenemunde), on the Baltic Sea island of Usedorn, 250 km north of Berlin, Germany, and reached 1.3 km • Germany occupies Egypt • Major General Dwight Eisenhower (1890 – 1969) is appointed commander of the US forces in Europe • the US air offensive against Germany begins • Netherland's government in exile (London) recognizes the Soviet Union • the first American offensive in Pacific starts at Guadalcanal, the principal island of the Solomon Islands, in the south-western Pacific, 1500 km northeast of Australia • Field Marshal Bernard Montgomery (1887 – 1976) becomes commandant of the British army in North Africa • British premier Churchill arrives in Moscow and meets Stalin • Dwight D Eisenhower is named commander for invasion of North Africa • Premier Churchill travels back to Cairo from Moscow • the US 8th Air Force bombs occupied Europe for the first time • Generalfeldmarschall Fredrich Paulus (1890 – 1957, married Elena Rosetti-Solescu in 1912 (she died in 1949, in Baden)) orders German 6th Army to conquer Stalingrad • Brazil declares war on Germany, Japan and Italy • the Battle of Stalingrad starts: 600 German Luftwaffe's bomb Stalingrad and 40,000 die • Cuba declares war on Germany, Japan and Italy • Germany annexes Luxembourg • German troops enter Stalingrad • Japanese planes drop incendiary bombs on Oregon, north of California, USA • British troops land on the island of Madagascar, 500 km east of Mozambique in southeast Africa • Russian troops organize a counter offensive at Stalingrad • launch of the first A-4/V-2 rocket to the altitude of 85 km takes place in Germany • the first salvo of the Russian Katjoesja-rocket destroys a German battalion in Stalingrad • the US and British governments announce the establishment of the United Nations • the first WW II American expeditionary force lands in Africa • last Vichy-French troops in Algeria surrender (Vichy is 400 km south of Paris) • 1 million Russians breach the German lines • 3rd and 5th Romanian army corps surrender • German 4th and 6th Army are surrounded at Stalingrad • Japan bombs again the Port Darwin, in the north of Australia • Josip Broz Tito (1892 – 1980) appoints Anti-fascist Liberation Committee in Yugoslavia • the first controlled nuclear chain reaction is done by the Italian physicist Enrico Fermi (1901 – 1954) at the University of Chicago • Solzhenitsyn, 24, is an artillery captain in the Russian army for 2.5 years during World War II.

Churchill's quote: *Courage is rightly esteemed the first of human qualities... because it is the quality which guarantees all others.*

415 BC. Plato is 13 years old.

Shortly before the departure of Athens' military expedition to Sicily, Athenian orator and politician, Andocides (440 BC – 390 BC), is imprisoned on suspicion of having taken part in the mutilation of the sacred busts called "Hermae" These mutilations cause a general panic, and Andocides is convinced to turn informer, and he implicates Alcibiades and others, who are condemned to death. Andocides is sent into exile.

The Athenian expedition to Sicily sets sail under Nicias, Lamachus and Alcibiades. After his departure with the armada, Alcibiades is accused of profanity and is recalled to Athens to stand trial. After learning that he has been condemned to death *in absentia*, Alcibiades defects to Sparta, and Nicias is placed in charge of the Sicilian expedition. The Athenian forces land at Dascon near Syracuse but with little success.

Alcibiades joins with the Spartans and persuades them to send Gylippus to assist Syracuse. He also encourages Ionia to revolt against Athens. As a result, a Spartan fleet soon arrives to reinforce their allies in Syracuse, and a stalemate results.

Plato's quote: *The excessive increase of anything causes a reaction in the opposite direction.*

1943. John is 14 years old. He, occasionally, cycles out to King's Somborne (a village in Hampshire, on the east edge of the valley of the River Test, 15 km west of Winchester) to visit his cousins Priscilla and Evelyn Dobbs, and their parents.

The US and Britain relinquish extraterritorial rights in China • Roosevelt and Churchill confer in Casablanca (the largest city in the western Morocco, on the Atlantic Ocean, 300 km southwest of Gibraltar) concerning WW II • the world's largest office building, with air conditioning system, the Pentagon (for the US Department of Defense), was completed • pre-sliced bread sale is banned in the US, to reduce bakery demand for metal parts • Soviets announce that they broke the long German siege of Leningrad (now Saint Petersburg, in the east of the Gulf of Finland in the Baltic Sea, 300 km east of Helsinki), where over one million city residents died • the US ration bread and metal • the Battle of Anzio (a small city on the Tyrhenian Sea, in the southwest Italy, 56 km south of Rome) takes place and Allies are stopped on the beach, by the Germans, until 1944 • British 8th army marches into Tripoli, Libya • Field Marshal Friedrich von Paulus surrenders to the Russian troops at Stalingrad and the battle of Stalingrad ends with the final surrender of the German 6th Army • shoe rationing begins in the US • Japanese evacuate Guadalcanal • The U.S. President Franklin Roosevelt, in an attempt to check inflation, freezes wages and prices, prohibits workers from changing jobs, unless the war effort would be aided thereby, and bars rate increases to common carriers and public utilities • Soviet Union breaks contact with the Polish government exiled in London • 5th German Pantzer army surrenders in Tunisia • US 7th division lands on Attu, Aleutian Islands, the first US territory recaptured from Japanese troops • Axis forces in North Africa surrender • Stalin dissolves the Comintern (Communist International, founded by Lenin in 1919 • The United States Army contracts with the University of Pennsylvania's Moore School to develop the ENIAC computer • British troops invade Pantelleria, Italy, (a tiny island, the ancient Cossyra, 100 km southwest of Sicily, and 60 km east of the Tunisian coast) • Allies begin 10-day bombing on Hamburg, north Germany • the US forces land at Nassau Bay, near the small town Salamaua, Papua New Guinea, 800 km northeast of Australia • the Battle of Kursk (USSR, 400 km northeast of Kiev and 600 km southwest of Moscow) begins, involving 6,000 tanks • the US invasion fleet (96 ships) sails to Sicily, Italy, and US, British and Canadian forces invade Sicily (Operation Husky) • after 8 days of heavy fighting, the greatest tank battle in history ends with the USSR victory over

Germany at Kursk, where almost 6,000 tanks took part, and 2,900 were lost by Germany • the Royal Air Force (RAF) bombs Germany rocket base at Peenemunde • 500 allied air forces raid Rome, Italy • the US forces led by General George Patton liberate Palermo, northwest of Sicily, Italy (Patton had ivory grips of his Colt .45 pistols he kept on him at all times. He was kneeling in silent prayer every morning.) • Benito Mussolini is captured and dismissed as premier of Italy • during the Battle of Troina, (center-east of Sicily, 60 km northwest of Catania), Mount Etna (3350 m, 40 km east of Troina) erupts, sending ash and lava many kilometers into the sky • Japan leaves Aleutian Islands, west Alaska, USA • German occupiers impose 72-hour work (over 10 hours/day, all days) week in occupied countries • Lord Mountbatten (1900 – 1979) is appointed Supreme Allied Commander in South East Asia • British 8th army lands in south Italy at Messina (Sicily) • Italy surrenders to the Allies in WW II • US, British and French troops land in Salerno (city on the Gulf of Salerno on the Tyrrhenian Sea, 50 km southeast of Naples (Napoli), Italy) (operation Avalanche) • German troops occupy Rome and take over the protection of the Vatican City • having been Generalissimo since 1928, Chiang Kai-shek becomes president of China • Great Britain establishes bases on the Archipelago of the Azores, in the North Atlantic Ocean, 1360 km west of Portugal • Italy declares war on its former Axis partner Germany • streptomycin, the first antibiotic remedy for tuberculosis, is isolated by researchers at Rutgers University, New Brunswick, New Jersey, USA • the first US ambassador to Canada, Ray Atherton (1883 – 1960), is nominated • 444 British bombers attack Berlin, Germany • US forces land on Tarawa and Makin Atoll in the Gilbert Islands (in the central Pacific Ocean, 3500 km northeast of Australia, and 4000 km southwest of Hawaii) • Roosevelt, Churchill and Chiang Kai-shek meet to discuss ways to defeat Japan • Lebanon declares independence from the French administration • Conference of Teheran (Iran, 1190 m, 100 km south of the Caspian Sea, 1600 km southeast of Stalingrad (now Volgograd)) between Churchill, Roosevelt and Stalin, takes place • the second conference of Cairo, Egypt: Roosevelt, Churchill and Turkish president Inonu (1884 – 1973), takes place • Roosevelt appoints General Eisenhower the supreme commander of the Allied forces in Europe.

Churchill's quote: *All the great things are simple, and many can be expressed in a single word: freedom, justice, honor, duty, mercy, hope.*

414 BC. Plato is 14 years old.
Athens sends out 73 vessels to Sicily, under the command of Demosthenes, to assist with the siege of Syracuse. The Athenian army moves to capture Syracuse, while the larger fleet of Athenian ships blocks the approach to the city from the sea. After some initial success, the Athenian troops become disorganized in the chaotic night operation, and are overpowered by Gylippus, the Spartan commander. The Athenian commander Lamachus is killed. Nicias, although ill, is left in sole charge of the siege of Syracuse.
Plato's quote: *There are two things a person should never be angry at, what they can help, and what they cannot.*

1944. John is 15 years old.
The first use of helicopters during warfare (British Atlantic patrol) takes place • the US Air Force announces the production of the first US jet fighter, the Bell P-59 • the first mobile electric power plant is delivered in Philadelphia, USA • Churchill and de Gaulle begin a two-day wartime conference in Marrakesh (major city in southeast Morocco, 600 km southwest of Gibraltar) • British Royal Air Force drops 2300 tons of bombs on Berlin • 447 German bombers attack London • 649 British bombers attack Magdeburg (an old medieval city on the Elbe River, 160 km southwest of Berlin, Germany) • Leningrad is liberated from the German blockade, after 880 days, with over 1,000,000 civilians killed • 683 British bombers attack Berlin • 285 German bombers attack London • Italian town of Cassino, 2 km east of Monte Cassino, destroyed by Allied bombing • Germany occupies Hungary • Mount Vesuvius (1281 m, 9 km east of Naples, Italy) erupts (the last eruption so far) • Japanese troops conquer Jessami, a small village in East-India, elevation 1200 m • the Soviet Army marches into Romania • British troops capture Addis Ababa, Ethiopia, from Italians • De Gaulle forms a new govern in exile • Allies bomb Bucharest, targeting railroads, and kill 5,000 people • Generals Rommel, Speidel and von Stulpnagel attempt to assassinate Hitler • the Polish 2nd Army corp captures the convent of Monte Cassini, Italy

- the German defense line in Italy collapses • Icelandic voters sever all ties with Denmark • the Japanese advance in Hangzhou, China, northwest of the Qiantang River, 150 km southwest of Shanghai • the Germans pull out of Rome, Italy • the US 5th Army enters and liberates Rome from Mussolini's Fascist armies • King Victor Emmanuel III of Italy (1869 – 1947) abdicates the power and then the throne for his son Umberto II (1904 – 1983, last king of Italy (only for 34 days)) • D-Day: 150,000 Allied Expeditionary Force lands in Normandy, France • the Russian offensive in Karelia (on the border with Finland) takes place • 15 US aircraft carriers attack Japanese bases on Marianas Islands (2000 km southeast of Japan, west of the Mariana Trench, the deepest part of the oceans (-10971 m) • the first German V-1 rocket assault on London takes place • the first B-29 bomber raid against mainland Japan takes place • the US forces begin the invasion of Saipan (part of the Northern Mariana Islands in Pacific, 2500 km south east of Japan) • Iceland declares independence from Denmark • Japanese troops conquer Changsha (on Xiang River, a branch of the Yangtze River, 900 km southwest of Shanghai, China) • the US Congress charters the Central Intelligence Agency • more than 2500 people are killed in London and South-East England by German V-1 flying bombs • the United Nations Monetary and Financial Conference (1 – 22 July 1944, 730 delegates from 44 Allied nations) at Bretton Woods (12 km west of Mount Washington (1917 m), 250 km north of Boston, USA) starts, establishing the International Monetary Fund and the World Bank. The Bretton Woods system worked for 27 years, until 1971

Mount Washington Resort, Bretton Woods, New Hampshire, USA, where the United Nations Monetary and Financial Conference took place in July 1944.

• the British troops march into Caen (northwest of France, 20 km south of the English Channel, 400 km west of Paris) • the US government recognizes the authority of General De Gaulle • Vilnius (200 km northwest of Minsk) , the capital of Lithuania (south of Latvia, northeast of Poland, west of Russia (now Belarus), is liberated by the Russian troops, which also cross the river Bug, the border with Poland •) • the first German V-2 rocket hits Great Britain • the first British jet fighter is used in combat (Gloster Meteor) • Turkey breaks diplomatic relationship with Germany • British 8th army reaches the suburbs of Florence (central Italy, 300 km northwest of Rome) • IBM dedicates, in the US, the first program-controlled calculator, the Automatic Sequence Controlled Calculator (known best as the Harvard Mark I) • Churchill and Tito meet in Naples (200 km southeast of Rome, Italy) • Operation Anvil: Allies land on the French Mediterranean sea coast, to liberate Montpellier, Marseille, and Nice • Operation Dragoon: Allied troops land in Provence (southeast of France) • the Russian troops arrive at the Austrian border • the last Japanese troops are driven out of India • the Russian offensive arrives at Jassy and Kishinev, northeast of Romania • Allied troops capture Marseilles, France • King Mihai (Michael) of Romania (born 1921, king 1927 – 1930 and 1940 – 1947) orders his forces to cease fire against Allies and dismisses the pro-Axis premier, Marshal Ion Antonescu (1882 – 1946) • a tank division of the British Guards frees Brussels, capital of Belgium, 300 km northeast of Paris • Finland breaks diplomatic contact with Germany • Belgium, Luxembourg and Netherlands sign unity treaty • the first German V-2 rockets land in London and Antwerp (Belgium, 50 km north of Brussels) • Russians march into Bulgaria and Bulgaria declares war on Germany • Allied forces liberate Luxembourg • Roosevelt and Churchill meet in Canada at the second Quebec Conference • • British troops land on Greek territory • Canadians free Austria • Soviets march into Hungary and Czechoslovakia • British Prime Minister Winston Churchill arrives in the USSR for talks with Stalin • US takes the Japanese island Okinawa (1500 km southwest of Tokyo) • Tannu Tuva (south of Russia, northwest of Mongolia) is annexed by the U.S.S.R. • German army retreats from Athens, Greece • Allied troops land in Corfu (western Greece, 100 km southeast of Italy) • British troops march into Athens, Greece • John Hopkins hospital in the USA performs the first open heart surgery • General De Gaulle arrives in Moscow • British order to disarm everybody in Greece, causes general strike there • the Greek Civil War breaks out in a newly-liberated Greece, between communists and royalists • Japanese-Americans are released from the detention camps in the US (in 1988 President Ronal Reagan (1911 – 2004) signed a law which apologized for the internment and paid over $1.6 billion in reparations) • Battle of Bastogne (city in southwest Belgium, at the border with Luxembourg): Germans surround the US 101st Airborne • The US Gen Patton's 4th Tank division turns away the German army at Bastogne • Budapest, Hungary, is surrounded by the Soviet army • King George II of Greece (1890 – 1947, spouse Elisabeth of Romania) abdicates his throne • Hungary declares war on Germany.

Churchill's quote: *The price of greatness is responsibility.*

413 BC. Plato is 15 years old.

Demosthenes wants to give up the siege of Syracuse and return to Athens, but Nicias refuses. The Syracusans and Spartans under Hermocrates are able to trap the Athenians in the harbor and the Athenians sustain heavy losses in the Battle of Syracuse. Demosthenes surrenders. Nicias is soon captured as well, and both are executed, with most of the surviving Athenian soldiers sent to work in the Sicilian mines.

Tissaphernes, the Persian satrap of Lydia and Caria, forms an alliance with Sparta. The Spartans, with strategic advice from Alcibiades and limited assistance from the Persians under Pharnabazus, advance almost to the gates of Athens. King Agis II leads the Spartan force that occupies Decelea (12 km north of Athens) in Attica.

Archelaus I becomes King (413 BC – 399 BC) of Macedonia following the death of his father, King Perdiccas II (451 BC – 413 BC).

Plato's quote: *Thinking: is the talking of the soul with itself.*

1945. John is 16 years old.
British Premier Winston Churchill visits France • Greek General Plastiras (1883 – 1953) forms a new government • the US aircraft carriers attack the Japanese island Okinawa (600 km southwest of the main Japan) • US soldiers led by General Douglas MacArthur (1880 – 1964) invade Philippines • German forces in Belgium retreat in the Battle of Bulge • the Soviets begin a large offensive against the Germans in Eastern Europe • the liberation of Warsaw by the Soviet troops takes place • Roosevelt, Churchill and Stalin meet at Yalta (a Russian resort city in the south of the Crimean peninsula, on the north coast of the Back Sea, 30 km east of Sevastopol, 500 km east of Constanta (Romania)) • US troops under General Douglas MacArthur enter Manila, Philippines • Russian Red Army crosses the river Oder, which forms part of the border between Poland and Germany, in the middle being 100 km east of Berlin • the US 76th and 5th Infantry divisions begin crossing river Sauer, which is in Belgium, Luxemburg and Germany, a left tributary of the river Moselle, and forms a part of the border between Luxemburg and Germany, 200 km west of Frankfurt • Allied planes bomb Dresden, in eastern Germany, 200

km south of Berlin, 135,000 die • the USSR captures Budapest (capital of Hungary, 300 km southeast of Vienna, Austria), after 49-day battle with German troops: 159,000 die • Peru, Paraguay, Chile and Ecuador join the United Nations • Venezuela declares war on Germany • 30,000 US Marines land on the Japanese island Iwo Jima (Sulfur Island, only 21 km^2, 1200 km south of Tokyo) • Queen Wilhelmina (1880 – 1962) returns to the Netherlands • Würzburg, central Germany (100 km southeast of Frankfurt), is 90% destroyed, with 5,000 dead, in only 20 minutes, by British bombers • 1,250 US bombers attack Berlin • Hitler issues the Nero Decree to destroy all German factories • the first Japanese flying bombs (ochas) attack US Navy ships near the Japanese island Okinawa (1500 km southwest of Tokyo) • the largest operation in the Pacific war: 1,500 US Navy ships bomb Okinawa, Japan • the Japanese resistance ends on Iwo Jima • the US 20th Army corp captures Wiesbaden, central Germany, on Rhein river, 20 km west of Frankfurt • the last German V-1 (buzz bomb) attack on London • the USSR invades Austria • the 32nd US President Franklyn D. Roosevelt dies (January 30, 1882 – April 12, 1945) • Harry Truman (1884 – 1972) is sworn in as the 33rd President of the USA • the Red Army occupies Wien (Vienna), Austria • American planes bomb Tokyo and damage the Imperial Palace • the US 7th Army and allies forces capture Nuremberg and Stuttgart in southern Germany • the Red Army begins the Battle of Berlin • Benito Mussolini flees from Salò (a small town on the central-west banks of Lago di Garda, 100 km east of Milano), to Milano • delegates from 46 countries gather in San Francisco for the United Nations Conference on International Organization • the last Boeing B-17 attack against Germany takes place • the Red Army completely surrounds Berlin • the US and Soviet forces meet at Torgau, Germany, on the Elbe River, 200 km southwest of Berlin • Marshal Henri Philippe Pétain (1856 – 1951), leader of France's Vichy collaborationist regime during WW II, is arrested for treason • • Italian partisans capture and execute Benito Mussolini (July 29, 1883 – April 28, 1945) • the US 5th army enters Genoa, northwest Italy, port on the Ligurian Sea, 150 km south of Milano • the Völkischer Beobachter, the newspaper of the Nazi Party in Germany, ceases publication • the US 5th army reaches the Swiss border • the Japanese army evacuates Rangoon in Burma (now

Yangon in Myanmar, 300 km west of Thailand) • the Terms of surrender of the German armies in Italy is signed • Admiral Karl Doenitz (1891 – 1980) forms a new German government • the Soviet army reaches Rostock, north Germany, on the Baltic Sea, 300 km northwest of Berlin • the German Army in Italy surrenders • the Soviet Union takes Berlin: General Weidling (1891 – 1955), the last commander of the Berlin Defense Area, surrenders, Adolf Hitler (April 20, 1889 – April 30, 1945) kills himself • Yugoslav troops occupy Trieste, seaport on the Adriatic Sea, in northeastern Italy, 150 km east of Venezia (Venice) • • German Field Marshal General Von Keitel (1882 – 1946) formally surrenders to the Russian Marshal Zhukov (1896 – 1974) • Victory in Europe Day: Germany signs unconditional surrender, World War II ends in Europe • • German archipelago of Helgoland (170 ha), in the southeastern corner of the North Sea, 200 km northwest of Hamburg, surrenders to the British troops • the US, USSR, UK and France agree to split occupied Germany, and they declare supreme authority over Germany • The US forces defeat the Japanese forces in the Japanese island Okinawa • The United Nations Charter is signed by 50 nations in San Francisco, USA • The Polish Provisional government of National Unity is set up by the Soviets • Ruthenia, formerly in the eastern Czechoslovakia, becomes part of the USSR • the Labour Party wins the British parliamentary election • the liberation of the Philippines is officially declared •• the first test detonation of an plutonium bomb takes place at Trinity Site, Alamogordo (200 km south of Albuquerque), New Mexico, USA, on July 16, 1945 at 5:30 AM • Potsdam (25 km southwest of Berlin) Conference, with Truman, Stalin and Churchill, holds its first meeting • Declaration of Potsdam: USA, UK and China demand Japanese surrender, but the Japanese government disregards the ultimatum • Winston Churchill resigns as UK's Prime Minister. Clement Attlee (1883 – 1967, PM 1945 – 1951, FRS) • the US Senate ratifies the United Nations charter 89-2 • the atomic bomb is dropped on Hiroshima (western Japan, 800 km southwest of Tokyo) on Aug 6th, to force Japan to surrender • the US, USSR, England and France sign the Treaty of London regarding the International Military Tribunal •• the USSR declares war against Japan and then establishes a communist government in North Korea • the USA drop the second atomic bomb on Japan and destroy part of Nagasaki (western Japan, 1000 km southwest of Tokyo, 300 km southwest of Hiroshima) • Japan announces willingness to surrender to Allies, provided that the status of 124th Emperor Hirohito (1901 – 1989, Emperor for 63 years) remains unchanged • Allies refuse Japan's surrender offer to retain the Emperor Hirohito unchanged • Victory on Japan Day: Japan surrenders unconditionally • South Korea is liberated from the Japanese rule • Aisin-Gioro Puyi (1906 – 1967), the last Emperor of China (the twelfth and final ruler of the Quig dynasty) and ruler of Manchukuo, is captured by the Soviet troops • Indonesia (Dutch East Indies) declares independence from the Netherlands • at the proposal of the US President Truman, Korea is divided on the 38th parallel, with the US occupying the southern area, and the USSR the northern area • Russian troops occupy Harbin (northeast China, 1200 km northeast of Beijing) and Mukden (now Shenyang, northeast China, 600 km northeast of Beijing, and 600 km southwest of Harbin) • the Vietnam conflict begins as Ho Chi Minh (1890 – 1969) leads a successful coup, British troops liberate Hong Kong (southern coast of China, at the South China Sea, 2000 km south of Beijing) from Japan • General MacArthur (1880 – 1964) is named the Supreme Commander of the Allied Powers in Japan • • the formal surrender of Japan takes place aboard USS Missouri, and the World War II ends • the first "bug" in a computer was discovered, a moth was removed with tweezers from a relay and taped into the log • Kim Il Sung (1912 – 1994) arrives in harbor of Wonsan, port of North Korea, on the westernmost shore of the Sea of Japan, 150 km east of Pyongyang • German rocket engineers begin work in the US • the US President Harry Truman announces that the atomic bomb secret was shared with Britain and Canada • the Chinese civil war begins, between Chiang Kai-Shek (1887 – 1975) and Mao Tse-Tung (1893 – 1976) • John Birch (1918 – 1945) US missionary and military intelligence officer in China is killed by the Communists (he was 27) • Juan Peron (1895 – 1974) becomes dictator of Argentina • Japanese troops surrender Taiwan to General Chiang Kai-Shek • General Enver Hoxha (1908 – 1985) becomes leader of Albania for 40 years • UNESCO is founded • General George C Marshall (1880 – 1959) is named special US envoy to China • Yugoslavian

Socialist Republic is proclaimed • the microwave oven is patented in the US • the Austrian Republic is re-established •

The International Monetary Fund is established and the World Bank is founded • the US Congress officially recognizes the "Pledge of Allegiance" • the Ratification of the United Nations Charter is completed.

Sweden runs a clandestine nuclear weapons program, to protect themselves against the Soviet Union.

The elder sister of J.R. Lucas - Ann

Lucas family celebrated the end of the war by going, with their 18 years old car, to Consett (town in the northwest of County Durham, which sits high on the edge of the Pennines, 20 km northwest of Durham), and the car achieved 45 mph (at which speed the needle is exactly vertical) on the way back to Durham, down a long straight gentle slope. It was at that period that the car got its name. It was, somehow, a benign anomaly in the English Constitution. In 1945 there was a General Election, and the two Houses of Convocation, one for each Province of the Established Church, were deemed to be part of Parliament, and were dissolved with the other elected House. Lucas' father was a member of the Northern Convocation, *ex officio*, by reason of being an Archdeacon. He was therefore granted 19 gallons extra of petrol so as to be able to canvas his supposed constituents. This meant that the family could go to visit Hexham (a market town and civil parish in Northumberland, near Hadrian's Roman Wall (122, the Romans had conquered the whole of Britain, but many Roman soldiers in northern Britain were dispatched to Dacia (now Romania), to deal with a rebellion, therefore this wall had to be built), south of the River Tyne, 50 km northwest of Durham), which has a jolly good abbey (built around 1150, though not as good as Durham Cathedral (1093)). While the car was parked outside, the Archdeacon was walking behind two workmen further down the street, and overheard one of them saying to the other ``My! Look at that piece of Old England''', and the car has been called that ever since. Later that day Lucas family was met by ironic cheers from a crowd returning from an event. In the car's back was Eric James (1909 – 1992, wrote the book "Plato's Ideas on Art and Education"), who had been John's chemistry master, and was going to be High Master of Manchester Grammar School. He stood up, and started bowing to them, and the crowd, having seen many films of triumphant entries into Paris, Brussels and Amsterdam, concluded that he really was someone important, cheered still, but respectfully. They were right. Later, as Sir Eric James, he helped found the University of York, and later still, as Lord James of Rusholme, he used to go up to the House of Lords ``in order to meet my former pupils''. It was tight fit: besides three in the back, there were three in the front, because the future Lady James was very thin, and could be squeezed in next the driver.

Solzhenitsyn, 27, is arrested for "disrespectful remarks" written about Stalin in correspondences with a friend. He is taken to a labor camp in Russia for an eight-year sentence.

Churchill's quote: *A man does what he must - in spite of personal consequences, in spite of obstacles and dangers and pressures - and that is the basis of all human morality.*

412 BC. Plato is 16 years old.

The Persians under Darius II want to recover control of the Greek cities of Asia Minor, which have been under Athenian control for 37 years, since 449 BC. The satraps of Asia Minor are ordered to collect overdue tribute.

The Spartans sign a treaty of mutual help with the Persian satrap of Lower Asia, Tissaphernes. By the treaty of Miletus, Persia is given complete freedom in western Asia Minor in return for agreeing to pay for seamen to man the Peloponnesian fleet.

Alcibiades helps stir up revolts amongst Athens' allies in Ionia, on the west coast of Asia Minor, but loses the confidence of the Spartans, and flees to the court of the Persian satrap Tissaphernes. Alcibiades advises Tissaphernes to withdraw his support from Sparta, while conspiring with the oligarchic party in Athens. The Athenians vote to use their last reserves to build a new fleet.

Plato's quote: *Those who wish to sing always find a song.*

1946. John is 17 years old, and much given to arguing, and in an argument with an opponent, his key Gödelian argument against determinism is presented. He writes later:: "The key manoeuvre came to me when I was seventeen at a meeting of the Essay Society where my arch-enemy Hugh Storey had read an essay putting forward an extreme reductionist view of the world---I still remember one phrase about wood-lice ``all that they can do is to curl up and micturate". I pointed out that he had been arguing for his reductionist world-view on the grounds that it was true, thus belying his thesis that we had no concept of truth, and what we believed we believed not because it was true, but because of the concatenation of determining factors in our physiology and environment."

The family of his cousins Priscilla and Evelyn Dobbs moves to Iffley Rectory (3 km southeast of Oxford).

The President of the British Academy is Sir Idris Bell (1879 – 1967, President 1946 – 1950, papyrologist (specializing in Roman Egypt) and scholar of Welsh literature)

The southeast side of the Mount Washington Resort, Bretton Woods, New Hampshire, USA, where the United Nations Monetary and Financial Conference took place in July 1944.

First meeting of United Nations General Assembly opens in London (Jan.10) • Winston Churchill's "Iron Curtain" speech warns of Soviet expansion. The Cold War begins. • The first automatic electronic digital computer, ENIAC, is dedicated at the University of Pennsylvania. • • The US Army makes radar contact with the Moon (400,000 km away) for the first time.

Churchill's quote: *Courage is what it takes to stand up and speak; courage is also what it takes to sit down and listen.*

The younger sister of J. R. Lucas - Sarah

411 BC. Plato is 17 years old, and begins to understand the important events around him.

On June 9 the democracy of Athens is overthrown by the aristocrats, Antiphon (480 BC – 411 BC), Theramenes (c 470 BC – 404 BC), Peisander and Phrynichus. A "Council of Four Hundred" is set up, but its rule is high-handed and the Council of Four Hundred is only able to maintain itself for four months.

When a mutiny breaks out amongst the troops who are fortifying Piraeus (the harbor for Athens), the Council sends Theramenes to quell it, but he puts himself at the head of the mutineers. After Phrynichus, the leader of the oligarchs, is assassinated, an ensuing meeting of the Athenian Assembly deposes the Council and restores the traditional constitution, but restricts some of the privileges of citizenship to a body called *the Five Thousand*.

The Athenian navy under Thrasybulus recalls Alcibiades (c 450 BC – 404 BC) from Sardis (in Persia, Asia Minor, 400 km east of Athens). Alcibiades' election is confirmed by the Athenians. A Spartan fleet in the Hellespont (means Sea of Helle, now called Dardanelles, a narrow strait (61 km long, 1.2 km to 6 km wide, 55 m average deep) connecting the Aegean Sea in the south to the Sea of Marmara in the north (which through the Bosphorus strait (31 km long, 0.7 km to 3.4 km wide, 13 m to 110 m depth, Istanbul is on both sides, the world's narrowest strait used for international navigation) connects to the Black Sea), and separating Europe (the Gallipoli peninsula to the west) from Asia (Asia Minor (Anatolia) to the east)) at Cynossema (a city where the Hellespont is only 1.2 km wide) is then defeated by an Athenian fleet commanded by Thrasybulus and Alcibiades.

Antiphon defends himself in a speech Thucydides (c 460 BC – c 400 BC, historian) describes as the greatest ever made by a man on trial for his life, but he is executed for treason.

Euripides' (c 480 BC – c 406 BC) play *Iphigenia in Tauris* is performed. Aristophanes' (c 446 BC – c 386 BC) plays *Lysistrata* and *Women Celebrating the Thesmophoria* are performed.

Plato's quote: *Those who intend on becoming great should love neither themselves nor their own things, but only what is just, whether it happens to be done by themselves or others.*

1947. John is 18 years old, and in June, together with his erstwhile enemy Hugh Storey, published an ephemeral magazine called ``Silly Point", which proved sufficiently profitable for him to buy (with some help from his father) a motorbike.

John finishes Winchester College and attends on a scholarship Balliol College, founded in 1263, one of the constituent colleges of the University of Oxford. He studies first mathematics, then Literae Humaniores (or Greats – an undergraduate course focused on Classics (Ancient Rome, Ancient Greece, Latin, ancient Greek and philosophy)), for 4 years, until 1951.

February 10: peace treaties for Italy, Romania, Bulgaria, Hungary, and Finland are signed in Paris. . • On March 12 the Truman Doctrine proposes "containment" of communist expansion. • In June the Marshall Plan is proposed to help European nations recover economically from World War II.

Solzhenitsyn, 29, begins using a post as a school teacher of mathematics and physics, inside the scientific labor camps in Russia, as a cover to write. "The First Circle" would later chronicle this time period.

Churchill's quote: *A pessimist sees the difficulty in every opportunity; an optimist sees the opportunity in every difficulty.*

410 BC. Plato is 18 years old.
Birth of Socrates' son Sophroniskos.

The Athenian fleet defeats the Spartan navy and its supporting Persian land army near Cyzicus (400 km northeast of Athens) on the south shore of the Propontis (Sea of Marmara), and Athens regains control over the vital grain route from the Black Sea.

Alcibiades installs a garrison at Chrysopolis (on the southeast part of the Bosphorus strait, now part of Istanbul), under Theramenes, to exact a tithe from all shipping that comes from the Black Sea. This revenue enables the Athenians to put an end to the regime of the Five Thousand and restore their traditional institutions in full. Democracy is restored in Athens. The new demagogue Cleophon (c 460 BC – 405 BC, mentioned in Aristotle's (384 BC – 322 BC) Rhetoric) dismisses peace overtures made by Sparta.

An Aristocratic revolt in Corcyra (now Corfu, an island in the east of the Ionian Sea, near Greece, 400 km northwest of Athens) is unsuccessful.

Carthage's Iberian colonies (now in Spain) revolt and secede. Hannibal Mago, the grandson of the Carthaginian general Hamilcar (who unsuccessfully invaded Sicily in 480 BC), begins preparations to reclaim Sicily.

Hippocrates of Chios, Greek Mathematician and Astronomer, passes away at 60 (c 470 BC – 410 BC).

Plato's quote: *A hero is born among a hundred, a wise man is found among a thousand, but an accomplished one might not be found even among a hundred thousand men.*

J. R. Lucas (right) and M. Dediu on November 3, 2006, at the International Conference "John Stuart Mill, 1806 – 2006".

1948. John is 19 years old, gets a First in Mathematical Moderations, and switches to Greats. He writes later: "I first heard of Gödel's theorem in 1948, when I was changing to Greats."

Once, on Shotover Hill (5 km east of Oxford, its highest point is 170 m), Lucas had, in his 21 years old car, eight boys from New College School (1379, independent preparatory school for boys in Oxford) for a birthday party. A police van drew up, and was prepared to be disapproving, but after being shown that the car's indicator lights were in working order, went away, satisfied.

At the end of February, Communists seize power in Czechoslovakia. . • Edwin Land (1909 – 1991, US) invents the Polaroid Land camera.

Churchill's quote: *A politician needs the ability to foretell what is going to happen tomorrow, next week, next month, and next year. And to have the ability afterwards to explain why it didn't happen.*

409 BC. Plato is 19 years old.

Alcibiades recaptures Byzantium (on the west side of the Bosphorus strait, colonized by Greek colonists from Megara (30 km west of Athens, 550 km from Byzantium) in 657 BC, then Constantinople (the capital city of the Eastern Roman Empire (330–1204 and 1261–1453), the Latin (1204–1261), and the Ottoman (1453–1924) empires. It was re-inaugurated in 324 at ancient Byzantium, as the new capital of the Roman Empire by Emperor Constantine the Great (272 – 337, 57th Emperor of the Roman Empire 306 – 337), after whom it was named, and dedicated on 11 May 330) and now Istanbul (from 1930)) , ending the city's rebellion against Athens. This action completes Athenian control of the Bosporus, which secures the Athenian supply route for grain from the Bosporus Kingdom in the Black Sea region.

The Athenian general Thrasyllus, sails out from Athens with a sizable force to campaign in Ionia (part of Asia Minor near Aegean Sea, around current Izmir, 350 km east of Athens). There, he quickly captures Colophon (50 km northeast of the Samos Island, 300 km east of Athens), and raids the Ionian countryside, but he is defeated outside Ephesus (3 km southwest of current Selcuk, 70 km northeast of the Samos Island, 320 km east of Athens, famous for the Temple of Artemis (550 BC, one of the Seven Wonders of the Ancient World)) by a combined Ephesian, Persian, and Syracusan force.

Pausanias (King 409 BC – 395 BC) succeeds his father Pleistoanax (King 458 BC – 409 BC) as Agiad (dynasty 930 BC – 222 BC) king of Sparta (930 BC – 192 BC, when it was annexed by the Achaean League (northern and central Peloponnese), then conquered by the Roman Republic in 146 BC).

The city of Rhodes is founded, on the Island of Rhodes, in the southeastern part of the Aegean Sea, 450 km southeast of Athens. It will become famous for the Colossus of Rhodes (280 BC, a statue of the Greek titan-god of the Sun Helios, one of the Seven Wonders of the Ancient World).

Plato's quote: *All things will be produced in superior quantity and quality, and with greater ease, when each man works at a single occupation, in accordance with his natural gifts, and at the right moment, without meddling with anything else.*

1949. John is 20 years old, and a no-good garage in Sunderland (a city in North East England, 25 km northeast of Durham) could not be bothered to find the handle of the right hand back door of his car, and just cut off the end and put a stub on it. The windshield of the car is missing. It was much used in Guildford days on the way back from the sea, when those in the back were liable to feel the cold. But it was taken off in Durham---there was no opportunity of going to the sea---and got left behind when we moved down South.

On April 4 twelve nations sign the North Atlantic Treaty establishing NATO.

Churchill's quote: *Broadly speaking, the short words are the best, and the old words best of all.*

408 BC. Plato is 20 years old, and he becomes uncle. Speusippus is born in Athens, Greek philosopher (died 339 BC). He was the son of Eurymedon and Potone, a sister of Plato, therefore Plato's nephew. After Plato's death, Speusippus inherited the Academy and remained its head for the next eight years. However, following a stroke, he passed the chair to Xenocrates (396 BC – 314 BC, philosopher and mathematician). Although the successor to Plato in the Academy, he frequently diverged from Plato's teachings. He rejected Plato's Theory of Forms.

Alcibiades enters Athens in triumph after an absence of 7 years, and is appointed commander-in-chief with autocratic powers.

The Spartan admiral Lysander (c 460 BC – 395 BC) arrives at Ephesus in autumn and builds up a great fleet with help from the new Persian satrap, Cyrus.

At the Panhellenic gathering at Olympia (northwest of the Island of Peloponnesus, 200 km west of Athens), the philosopher Gorgias (c. 465 BC – c. 380 BC) speaks out against the Spartan alliance with Persia. Plato will be one of Gorgias' philosophy greatest critics. Aristotle will also criticize Gorgias philosophy.

Euripides' (c. 480 BC – c. 406 BC) plays *Orestes* and *The Phoenician Women* are performed. Euripides then leaves Athens in dissatisfaction, and travels to the court of Archelaus I of Macedon (King 413 BC – 399 BC) at the King's invitation.

Eudoxus of Cnidus (city on the west end of Datca peninsula on the southwestern Asia Minor, 80 km northeast of Rhodes, 330 km southeast of Athens) is born, Greek astronomer, mathematician, physician, student of Plato, scholar and adherent of Pythagoras (c. 570 BC – c. 495 BC, the greatest Ionian Greek philosopher and mathematician) (Eudoxus died c. 355 BC, at 53).

Pythagoras' quote: *Were it not for number and its nature, nothing that exists would be clear to anybody either in itself or in its relation to other things...You can observe the power of number exercising itself ... in all acts and the thoughts of men, in all handicrafts and music.*

1950. John is 21 years old, and, while he was driving his 23 years old car, the car's horn got stuck, and sounded continuously all the way up Northumberland Street, a major shopping street, west of Northumbria University, in Newcastle upon Tyne (a city in North East England, 20 km north of Durham, and 10 km northwest of Washington), to his great embarrassment. Since then Lucas has clearly understood that silence is often golden, and sounds the horn as little as he can.

The family celebration of John's 21th birthday took place in Iffley, at the family of his cousins Priscilla and Evelyn Dobbs.

The President of the British Academy is Sir Charles Kingsley Webster (1886 – 1961, President 1950 – 1954, historian and diplomat).

The first modern credit card Diners Club is introduced in the US. The Korean War begins.

Solzhenitsyn, 32, is transferred to a labor camp for political prisoners in Russia, where he contracts stomach cancer. It clears in

1954, at 36, after treatment. The ordeal is later published as "The Cancer Ward" and "The Right Hand".

Churchill's quote: *A lie gets halfway around the world before the truth has a chance to get its pants on.*

The central east side of the Mount Washington Resort, Bretton Woods, New Hampshire, USA, where the United Nations Monetary and Financial Conference took place in July 1944.

407 BC. Plato is 21 years old, meets Socrates (469 BC – 399 BC), 62 years old, and Plato abandons aspirations to be playwright.

In the Agora of Athens the great philosopher Socrates questioned the market-goers on their understanding of the meaning of life, attracting a crowd of Athenian youth. In this marketplace, one day in 407 BC, the young poet Aristocles, son of Ariston, heard Socrates speaking, then went and burned all his works, and became the philosopher known as Plato. His philosophical dialogues, coupled with his founding of the Academy, the first University, and his role as the teacher of Aristotle, who then was tutor to Alexander the Great, changed western philosophy. A contemporary of Plato's, Diogenes of Sinope (c 404 BC – 323 BC), lived in a tub in the Agora and followed Socrates' example of questioning the Athenians on their understanding of the more important aspects of life. Diogenes is well known for searching for an honest man (though, actually, he claimed he was searching for a real human being) by holding a candle or lantern to people's faces in the Agora.

The Spartan admiral Lysander refuses to be lured out of Ephesus to do battle with Alcibiades. However, while Alcibiades is away seeking supplies, the Athenian squadron is placed under the command of Antiochus, his helmsman, who is routed by the Spartan fleet (with the help of the Persians under Cyrus) in the Battle of Notium (or Ephesus).

The defeat gives the enemies of Alcibiades an excuse to strip him of his command. He never returns again to Athens. He sails north to land he owned in the Thracian Chersonese (now called the Gallipoli peninsula (Gallipoli comes from the Greek Kallipolis (Beautiful City))). Except for a brief appearance at Aegospotami (a small river northeast of Sestos, in the Thracian Chersonese, issuing into the Hellespont (now Dardanelle)) Alcibiades' involvement in the Peloponnesian War is over.

Pythagoras' quote: *The oldest, shortest words - "yes" and "no" - are those which require the most thought.*

1951 – Lucas receives a BA with 1st Class Honours in Greats, at Balliol College, Oxford.

Between 1951 and 1953 Lucas is Harmsworth Senior Scholar at Merton College, Oxford.

Prime Minister of the United Kingdom is again Sir Winston Churchill (1874 – 1965, PM for the second time 1951 – 1955, FRS).

Churchill's quote: *A joke is a very serious thing.*

406 BC. Plato is 22 years old.

Athenians defeat Spartan fleet at Arginusae: Socrates opposes subsequent charges against Athenian generals for failure to rescue survivors.

The Roman Republic forces begin a decade-long siege against Veii (an important Etruscan city 16 km northwest of Rome).

Euripides, Athenian playwright, born c. 480 BC, dies at 74.

Sophocles, Athenian dramatist and politician, b. c. 495 BC, dies at 89.

Sophocles' quote: *Time alone reveals the just man; but you might discern a bad man in a single day.*

1952 – Lucas receives John Locke (FRS, English philosopher and physician, 1632 – 1704) Scholarship at the University of Oxford.

On February 6, Princess Elizabeth of York, 25, becomes Elizabeth II, Queen of the United Kingdom, Canada, Australia, New Zealand, South Africa, Pakistan and Ceylon. On February 26, Elizabeth's Prime Minister, Winston Churchill, announces possession of an atomic bomb.

Churchill's quote: *Although personally I am quite content with existing explosives, I feel we must not stand in the path of improvement.*

405 BC. Plato is 23 years old.
Athens capitulates to the Spartans.
Sicily is mostly occupied by the Carthagians.
The *Erechtheum*, which includes *The Porch of Maidens* (Caryatid Porch), is completed in the Ionian style, on the Acropolis in Athens, after 16 years of construction.
Philolaus, Greek mathematician and philosopher, born circa 480 BC, dies at 75.

Pythagoras' quote: *As soon as laws are necessary for men, they are no longer fit for freedom.*

1953 – 1956: Lucas is elected to a Junior Research Fellowship at Merton College (1264, Collegium Mertonense, one of the constituent colleges of the University of Oxford). His father retired in 1953, and moved to Randolph's Steeple Aston (a village on the west edge of the Cherwell Valley in Oxfordshire, 15 km north of Oxford), which his mother had recently inherited from her uncle. In his retirement the father was Wiccamical Prebend of Chichester Cathedral until his death in 1958.

Stalin dies on March 5, 1953, at 74, after 30 years of dictatorship. On September 7 Nikita Khrushchev (1894 – 1971) takes power in the Soviet Union and starts some reforms.

Locke's quote: *All mankind... being all equal and independent, no one ought to harm another in his life, health, liberty or possessions.*

404 BC. Plato is 24 years old, and he was active politically (*Letter* 7). His uncle and cousin were among the Thirty Tyrants (404/3), who terrorized the Athenian state after Athens lost the war to Sparta. The Peloponnesian War ends. Athens' empire is dismantled.

All important Athenian statesmen are executed.

Darius II Ochus, King of the Persian Empire, dies.

Plato's quote: *Without effort, you cannot be prosperous. Though the land may be good, you cannot have an abundant crop without cultivation.*

1954 – Lucas receives a MA in Philosophy.

The President of the British Academy is Sir George Norman Clark (1890 – 1979, President 1954 – 1958, Professor of Economic History at the University of Oxford and Professor of Modern History at the University of Cambridge).

On February 19, the 1954 transfer of Crimea takes place: The Soviet Politburo of the Soviet Union orders the transfer the Crimean Oblast from the Russian SFSR to the Ukrainian SSR. On February 23 – The first mass vaccination of children against polio begins in Pittsburgh, United States. On February 25 – Lt. Col. Gamal Abdel Nasser (1918 – 1970) becomes premier of Egypt.

Locke's quote: *Government has no other end, but the preservation of property.*

403 BC. Plato is 25 years old, and he turns away from politics, toward philosophy.

Socrates' son Menexenos was born in 402 BC.

Athens restores some democratic institutions, after some battles. Also the Euclidean alphabet is introduced.

In China starts the Warring States period. Some rulers support Confucianism.

Confucius' quote: *Do not impose on others what you yourself do not desire.*

1955 – Lucas invited to apply for a Research Lectureship at Christ Church (which did not want to elect A.M. Quinton), but declined, partly because he in turn did not want to be colleagues with Dundas or Trevor Roper, and chiefly because he still had a year of his Junior Research Fellowship at Merton".

Prime Minister of the United Kingdom is Sir Anthony Eden (1897 – 1977, PM 1955 – 1957, Suez Crisis, resigned due to ill health).

402 BC. Plato is 26 years old.
Archelaus I, King of Macedonia from 413 BC to 399 BC, helps establish a pro-Macedonian oligarchy in the capital Larissa of Thessaly, 220 km northwest of Athens.
Confucius' quote: *When a country is governed well, poverty and mean condition are things to be ashamed of. When a country is governed poorly, riches and honor are things to be ashamed of.*

J. R. Lucas (right) and M. Dediu on November 3, 2006, at the International Conference "John Stuart Mill, 1806 – 2006".

1956 – 1957: Lucas is Fellow and Assistant Tutor at Corpus Christi College (1352, a constituent college of the University of Cambridge).
In 1956 Lucas is invited to apply for a Tutorial Fellowship at New College, Oxford, but declines, having already committed himself to Corpus. A.M. Quinton is elected."

Much later Lucas writes:
"Going to Cambridge

In 1956 I went to Cambridge to see if I would do as Second Tutor of Corpus. .

As I now see it, there were a variety of different motives behind the invitation.

Corpus had had a crisis over the tutorship some years earlier, and Michael McCrum had been hooked out of Rugby to come and take over the running of the College.

He had done this extremely well, but had now become involved in university affairs, and had not got enough time to be a member of Council .and to take full pastoral care of all the undergraduates in College.

He wanted a pastoral assistant.

The Master and Fellows agreed, but wanted more. They foresaw Michael's being lured into a headmastership somewhere, and the College being bereft of tutorial timber. They wanted a Second Tutor, who would be a Tutor-in-waiting, ready to take over the tutorship when Michael departed. It was known I had read Greats, and it was widely believed that Greatsmen were super administrators, well prepared to take Top Jobs. It was also the case that the College had no supervisor in Moral Science (i.e. Philosophy), although Professor Thouless had been an eminent member of the Faculty.

The previous year Corpus had interviewed Robert Ogilvie, who had been suggested by Michael Foster of Christ Church, as a pastorally minded high-flyer, who was also a Christian (which both Michael and George Thomson, the Master, thought important), but he had not been found acceptable (and became a research Fellow of Clare, and then a tutorial fellow of Balliol).

Michael Foster must have been asked if there was anyone else he could suggest. It was generous of him to mention my name, since I had turned down Christ Church the previous year.

So Corpus came to hear of me, and invited me over.

I was interviewed first by the Master, George Thomson, who had won the Nobel Prize for showing that the electrons were not just particles, as his father, J.J. Thomson had won the Nobel Prize for proving, but were waves. He was an immensely impressive man. I started on the wrong foot, instancing fluid dynamics as the sort of research that was not fundamental. Fluid dynamics was George Thomson's first bit of research. But he forgave me. I noticed that in his portrait, which was on his left, the artist had included a reflection of it: G. P. said that the artist had put it in without thinking, and had then painted it out, but had been persuaded to put it in again.

I had lunch on cold mutton chops with George Carter (who had been temporary tutor during the crisis) and about eight bachelor fellows. I passed. Michael's first choice having been turned down, there was considerable reluctance to disappoint him again. So I was elected to be Second Tutor.

I had been due to go to Princeton for a year. Corpus asked Princeton to postpone it for a year, when I should have leave of absence for that year. So I spent 1956-7 in Corpus and 1957-8 in Princeton.

By the end of 1957, it was evident that I was not a great administrator, and would not do as Tutor. Two Assistant Tutors were appointed to help Michael McCrum during my absence, and on my return I was Assistant, not Second, Tutor, needing to get on ``the ladder" in due course if I was to obtain a university post, and stay on at Corpus as a proper university teacher. In retrospect I see this as something of a put-down, but it did not seem so at the time. I was quite happy for the future to take care of itself. And as it happened soon afterwards Braithwaite summoned me to his room in King's to tell me of a university post coming up in the History and Philosophy of Science, for which I would be an extremely well qualified candidate.

But it was not to be. My first girl-friend dumped me, and married a Fellow of Corpus.

It would have been unbearable to remain.
I went to Leeds."

. On January 17 – USS *Nautilus*, the first nuclear-powered submarine, puts to sea for the first time, from Groton, Connecticut. On January 18–January 20 – the Battle of Yijiangshan Islands (30 km east of the city Taizhou in China and 400 km north of Taipei in Taiwan) takes place: The Chinese Communist People's Liberation Army seizes the islands from the Republic of China (Taiwan).

A little known but important request from Syria for Soviet military assistance and intervention in 1956 – the USSR refused. This event provides a historical context behind Russia's involvement in the ongoing conflict in Syria 60 years later, in 2016.

Locke's quote: *Mens sana in corpore sano: A sound mind in a sound body, is a short, but full description of a happy state in this World: he that has these two, has little more to wish for; and he that wants either of them, will be little the better for anything else.*

401 BC. Plato is 27 years old.

Cyrus the Younger, the younger son of Darius II of Persia and Parysatis, who was a Persian prince, general, and governor of Asia Minor, died after a failed battle to oust his brother, Artaxerxes II, from the Persian throne, where he was King from 404 BC to 358 BC (46 years).

Plato's quote: *I never did anything worth doing by accident, nor did any of my inventions come by accident; they came by work.*

1957 – Lucas publishes 'The Soul' (in Basil G. Mitchell's 1957 collection *Faith and Logic*), where he defends the soul against Gilbert Ryle's reductive analysis. This work helped initiate the revival of the philosophy of religion in English-speaking philosophy.

Trinity College, Oxford, invites Lucas to apply for a Tutorial Fellowship, but Lucas declines, because his Corpus Fellowship gives him more time for thinking.'

On January 20, Dwight D. Eisenhower (1890 – 1969) is inaugurated for a second term as President of the United States. The first nuclear-powered submarine, the USS *Nautilus* (1954) logs its 60,000th nautical mile (111,120 km, 20,000 leagues), matching the endurance of the fictional *Nautilus* described in Jules Verne's (1828 – 1905) novel *"20,000 Leagues Under the Sea"* (1869). It is decommissioned on March 3, 1980.

Byron's quote: *If I don't write to empty my mind, I go mad.*

The east side of the Mount Washington Resort, with the Ammonoosuc River (down), Bretton Woods, New Hampshire, USA, where the United Nations Monetary and Financial Conference took place in July 1944.

400 BC. Plato is 28 years old.

War breaks out between Sparta and Elis (in the northwest of the Peloponnese Island).

The Carthaginians occupy Malta.

The catapult is invented by Greek engineers.

The mature classical period of sculpture ends in Ancient Greece

Dionysius I (c 432 BC – 367 BC), Greek tyrant of Syracuse, confiscates gold and silver coins, re-mints it keeping the weight the same, but changing the denomination from one to two drachmae — the first known official devaluation at the expense of the general population. A virulent inflation ensues.

Thucydides, Greek historian, born c. 460 BC, dies at 60.

Aspasia of Miletus, widow of Pericles of Athens (c. 495 BC – 429 BC, the most prominent and influential Greek statesman, orator and general of Athens during the Golden Age (480 BC – 404

BC, Age of Pericles is from 461 BC to 429 BC)) born c. 470 BC, dies. Her house was an intellectual center in Athens, attracting the most prominent writers and thinkers, including the philosopher Socrates (same age as Aspasia). Aspasia was mentioned in the writing of philosophers Plato, Aristophanes, Xenophon, and other authors of the day.

Thucydides' quote: *Ignorance is bold and knowledge reserved.*

1957- 1958 - Lucas spent this academic year, as a Visiting Fellow at Princeton University (1746, in New Jersey, USA, motto: Dei Sub Numine Viget (Under God's Power She Flourished), private Ivy League research university), where he studied mathematics and logic.

Prime Minister of the United Kingdom is Harold Macmillan (1894 – 1986, PM 1957 – 1963, FRS, resigned due to ill health).

Byron's quote: *It is very certain that the desire of life prolongs it.*

1958 – Lucas' father passes away.

The President of the British Academy is Sir Maurice Bowra (1898 – 1972, President 1958 – 1962, Warden of Wadham College, Oxford (1938 – 1970) and Vice-Chancellor of the University of Oxford (1951 – 1954)).

In the first day of 1958 the European Economic Community (EEC) is founded, and the first Carrefour store opens in Annecy, a city in south-eastern France, on the northern tip of Lac d'Annecy, 35 km south of Geneva, Switzerland. On December 18 the United States launches SCORE, the world's first communications satellite.

Mill's quote: *Every great movement must experience three stages: ridicule, discussion, adoption.*

The room in the Mount Washington Resort, Bretton Woods, New Hampshire, USA, where the documents of the United Nations Monetary and Financial Conference were signed in July 1944.

399 BC. Plato is 29 years old.

On February 15, the Greek philosopher Socrates (who taught in the court of the Agora of Athens, located below the Acropolis) is sentenced to death by Athenian authorities, condemned for impiety and the corruption of youth. He refuses to flee into exile and dies by drinking hemlock (born 470 BC, 71 years old). Plato was present at the trial, but not allowed to speak. Plato and other disciples removed themselves to Megara, next town west of Athens. There was later a 'Megarean School' of Socratic philosophy: Elkleides of Megara (author of a *Crito, Eroticus, Aeschines, Alcibiades)*, Bryson and Stilpo.

Sparta forces Elis to surrender in the spring.

King Amyrtaeus of Egypt (from 404 BC to October 399 BC) is defeated in battle by his successor, Nepherites I (398 BC – 393 BC) of Mendes, and executed at Memphis. King Nepherites I, or Nefaarud I, founds the Twenty-ninth dynasty of Egypt. He makes Mendes his capital.

Socrates' quote: *It is not living that matters, but living rightly.*

1959 – 1960 – Lucas is Leverhulme (foundation established in 1925 under the will of William Lever, 1st Viscount Leverhulme (1851 – 1925, industrialist and politician)) Research Fellow, at the University of Leeds (1904, motto: Et augebitur scientia (And knowledge will be increased), West Yorkshire, 60 km northeast of Manchester, 275 km north of London).

Lucas' cousins Priscilla and Evelyn Dobbs, and their parents, left Iffley in 1959.

Sweden is ready for underground testing of nuclear weapons, but Riksdag (Parliament) prohibited nuclear weapons.

Mill's quote: *A person may cause evil to others not only by his actions but by his inaction, and in either case he is justly accountable to them for the injury.*

398 BC. Plato is 30 years old, and goes to Megara, with other followers of Socrates.

Dionysius, tyrant of Syracuse, breaks his peace treaty with Carthage and strikes at Carthaginian cities in the western corner of Sicily, which have been weakened by the plague. Motya (on an island off the west coast of Sicily), with its good harbor, is attacked and captured.

Plato's quote: *Necessity... the mother of invention.*

Chapter 4: Lucas at Oxford

1960 - 1996 – Lucas at Oxford 1947-1996 -- Lucas starts his academic career at Balliol College, Oxford, where he was an undergraduate. He was supported by a Fraser Scholarship which he had been given in his last year at Winchester, and a Domus Exhibition, and initially by his father. In 1951 he is awarded a Harmsworth Senior Scholarship at Merton College, Oxford. In 1952 he wins the John Locke Scholarship for Mental Science, and in 1953, he is elected to a Junior Research Fellowship at Merton.

After a spell at Cambridge (see 1956) and Leeds (see 1959) he returns to Merton as a tutorial fellow in 1960, and remains there until his retirement in 1996,

Often during this time John visits his cousins Priscilla (11 years younger) and Evelyn Dobbs (13 years younger), and their parents in Iffley, using his motorbike. He tells his cousins many stories about cows.

The Chancellor of the University of Oxford is Harold Macmillan (1894 – 1986, Chancellor 1960 – 1986, Prime Minister 1957 - 1963).

Mill's quote: *All good things which exist are the fruits of originality.*

397 BC. Plato is 31 years old.

King Agesilaus II of Sparta launches a campaign in Asia Minor against the Persian King Artaxerxes II.

The Carthaginians establish the town of Lilybaeum (now Marsala in the westernmost part of Sicily) to replace Motya.

Himilco crosses to Sicily from Carthage with a fresh army, conquers the north coast, puts Dionysius I, the Tyrant of Syracuse, on the defensive, and besieges Syracuse. However, the Carthaginian army again suffers from the plague. The Syracusans counterattack and completely defeat Himilco's army. Himilco has to escape back to Carthage.

Plato's quote: *The beginning is the most important part of the work.*

1961 - Lucas publishes his best known paper, Minds, Machines and Gödel. He also helped found the Oxford Consumers' Group, and was its first chairman in 1961-1963, serving again in 1965.

Also, and much more important, Lucas, 32, was getting married.

Morar Portal (18, future wife of Lucas) in Florence (Firenze, Italy) in 1947. Lucas writes in 2016: "This photo was taken in Florence in

1947, and is of Morar Portal, as she then was. It was her first visit abroad, which she undertook with Mary Gibbs, who later was her bridesmaid, and Helen's Godmother. It is the photo of her I keep where I can see it when sitting in my chair in the library, and would be suitable in the book as picturing the wife I married."

Mrs. Morar Lucas (born 30 May 1929) is the elder daughter of Admiral Sir Reginald Henry Portal (1894 – 1983), DSC (Distinguished Service Cross), KCB (Knight Commander of the Order of the Bath), CB (Companion of The Most Honourable Order of the Bath), he served in Australia at the end of the war against Japan.

J. R. Lucas on November 3, 2006, at the International Conference "John Stuart Mill, 1806 – 2006".

Admiral Sir Reginald Portal (1894 – 1983).

Lady Portal, wife of Admiral Sir Reginald Portal

Viscount Portal of Hungerford, OM (Order of Merit), KG (Order of the Garter) Marshal of The Royal Air Force.

The newly married couple live at Grove Cottage, St Cross Road, Oxford.

Lucas' cousin Evelyn Dobbs is an undergraduate student at Oxford, and she visits John and Morar in their Rose Lane cottage.

Mill's quote: *All political revolutions, not affected by foreign conquest, originate in moral revolutions.*

396 BC. Plato is 32 years old, and publishes his Apologia, which is a defense of his mentor Socrates. Apologia is considered the beginning of the western philosophy.

Agesilaus II, the King of Sparta, campaigns successfully in Asia Minor against the Persian satraps Pharnabazus and Tissaphernes, and defeats Tissaphernes at Sardis.

Marcus Furius Camillus (c. 446 BC – 365 BC) is made dictator by the Romans. Camillus finally occupies the Etruscan city of Veii in southern Etruria after a 10 years siege. The capture of Veii and its surrounding territories marks the first major expansion of Rome, which doubles its territory after this victory. The Romans introduce pay for their army.

Xenocrates is born, Greek philosopher and scholarch (or rector) of the Academy (died 314 BC).

Plato's quote: *And what, Socrates, is the food of the soul? Surely, I said, knowledge is the food of the soul.*

1962 – One of Lucas' students writes these notes:

"Sunday 4th Nov. 1962. Today mass in chapel, then breakfast with Lucas at 9.00 a.m. - grapefruit, steak & tomatoes, toast, green butter & marmalade & coffee. Very interesting talk.

Friday 23rd Nov. Signed off dinner. Socratic Club: Lucas & Stead (Keble chaplain) on sin. Both very clear, the first discussion I have understood."

Lucas was 33 and his car 35. The car's autovac gave out again at the end of his father's Durham days, when they were on the famous Fosse (from fossa, Latin for ditch) Way (a magnificent 370 km Roman road built in Provincia Britannia (43 – 410) of the Roman Empire, which linked Isca Dumnoniorum (Exeter, 240 km southwest of London) to Lindum Colonia (Lincoln, 200 km north of London), via Lindinis (Ilchester, 120 km southwest of London), Aquae Sulis (Bath, 150 km west of London), Corinium (Cirencester,

120 km northwest of London), and Ratae Corieltauvorum (Leicester, 140 km northwest of London)). This time the autovac had to be replaced. Lucas, sometimes, had to use the starter a lot before there was enough petrol in the carburetor to make the engine fire. But that was a problem anyhow. To get a quick start, Mr. Lucas would squirt a little ether into one of the cylinders. It worked a treat, so much so that the car became addicted. The drivers had become addicted too, and when Mr. Lucas wanted to buy some more, he was told that it could no longer be bought without authorization. So he wrote out an authorization for him to buy solvent ether, signing it rather grandly ``J.R. Lucas, MA, Fellow of Merton College, Oxford", which was accepted as suitably authoritative

The President of the British Academy is The Lord Robbins (1898 – 1984, President 1962 – 1967, economist at the London School of Economics).

Mill's quote: *I have learned to seek my happiness by limiting my desires, rather than in attempting to satisfy them.*

395 BC. Plato is 33 years old and serves in the military.

The "Corinthian War" (395 BC – 387 BC) begins, with Athens, Thebes (northwest of Athens), Corinth (northeast of Peloponnese) and Argos (northeast of Peloponnese) (with the backing of Persia), against Sparta (south of Peloponnese).

Plato's quote: *For good nurture and education implant good constitutions.*

1963 - One of the more striking weekly events in Oxford (of probably 1963) consisted in a series of dialogues between J.R. Lucas and Alasdair MacIntyre, conducted in one of the halls of the Oxford Examination Schools building.

Prime Minister of the United Kingdom is Sir Alec Douglas-Home (1903 – 1995, PM 1963 – 1964).

On January 8, Leonardo da Vinci's (1452 in Vinci, Republic of Florence, now Italy – 1519 in Amboise, Kingdom of France) *Mona Lisa* (or la Gioconda, 1503 – 1507, Louvre, Paris, France) is exhibited in the United States for the first time, at the National Gallery of Art in Washington, D.C.

Mill's quote: *Life has a certain flavor for those who have fought and risked all, that the sheltered and protected can never experience.*

394 BC. Plato is 34 years old, and serves in the military.

Sparta wins some land battles, but Persia wins a naval battle and gains mastery of the Aegean Sea.

Plato's quote: *Ignorance, the root and stem of all evil.*

J. R. Lucas on November 3, 2006, at the International Conference "John Stuart Mill, 1806 – 2006".

The room in the Mount Washington Resort, Bretton Woods, New Hampshire, USA, where the documents of the United Nations Monetary and Financial Conference were signed in July 1944.

Basil Mitchell at Postmasters' Hall, one of the oldest houses in Oxford, on Merton Street. For many years Lucas family lived here.

1964

Prime Minister of the United Kingdom is Harold Wilson (1916 – 1995, PM 1964 – 1970, FRS).

On May 1, at 4:00 AM, John George Kemeny (1926 – 1992, mathematician, President of Dartmouth College (1769, Hanover (on the Connecticut River, 180 km northwest of Boston), New Hampshire, USA, Latin: Collegium Dartmuthensis, motto: Vox clamantis in deserto (The voice of one crying out in the wilderness))) and Thomas Eugene Kurtz (1928, mathematician, Professor at Dartmouth College) ran the first computer program written in BASIC (Beginners' All-purpose Symbolic Instruction Code), an easy to learn high level programming language which they created. BASIC was eventually included on many computers and even some games consoles.

Mill's quote: *War is an ugly thing, but not the ugliest of things. The decayed and degraded state of moral and patriotic feeling, which thinks that nothing is worth war, is much worse.*

393 BC. Plato is 35 years old. The First Period of Plato's literary activity is between 399 BC and 390 BC: *Laches, Protagoras, Apology, Charmides, Hippias Minor, Crito, Euthyphro, Ion, Gorgias, Lysis, and Hippias Major.*

The "Corinthian War" continues, with alternating victories.

In Egypt, King Nepherites I (398 BC – 393 BC) dies, Psammuthes becomes King for several months, and then Hakor (King 392 BC – 379 BC) overthrows him.

Aristophanes' (c. 446 BC – c. 386 BC, *the Father of Comedy* and *the Prince of Ancient Comedy*) play, a new comedy called "The Ecclesiazusae", is performed. Plato singled out Aristophanes' play "The Clouds" as slander that contributed to the trial and subsequent condemning to death of Socrates, although other satirical playwrights had also caricatured Socrates.

Socrates' quote: *By all means marry. If you get a good wife, you'll be happy. If you get a bad one, you'll become a philosopher.*

Mr. and Mrs. Lucas on November 3, 2006, at the International Conference "John Stuart Mill, 1806 – 2006".

1965 –Lucas serves again in Oxford Consumers' Group.

1st Dec. 1965 Oxford. From ECWB. ... Mulled claret & chestnuts with the Lucases - a very peaceful & interesting occasion... Penny was invited to mulled & chestnuts as well as me, so I was quite glad Clive & Stephen were there + 2yr. P.P.E. people: a most hateful person called Michael, who now has Callum's room, but otherwise everyone else v. agreeable... Mr. Lucas said how he missed hearing the late-night snatches of conversation wh. his undergraduate rms. had availed him of: one night he remembered hearing a man say in an undertone, "I'm desperately in --" & that was all. I thought of standing outside Grove Cottage & finishing the sentence - my way. Women can now dine on high table. Lucas is shattered & has no intention of taking Mrs. L. - who, Penny & I think, is having another baby.

1st Dec. (again) From ECWB. Petra (one of the nice English people) had a peaceful evening's baby-sitting on Friday. There were screams from Edward shortly after the Lucases had left, so Petra went up & put her head round his door, only to be told "I'm quite all right, thank you".

2nd Dec. Oxford. From ECWB. Mrs. Lucas asked me to baby-sit tonight, but I couldn't, so Penny went; yes, they are having another baby.

8th Dec. Durham. From JDH. How splendid about the Lucases' next child! Another nice person in the world.

11th Dec. Oxford. From ECWB. Penny & I were v. kindly asked to lunch with the Lucases (on Thurs.). The Chaplain was there, too.... Edward was very quiet at lunch. Asked to ask us if we would like sherry, he said "No, I'm too shy". He has been asking Mrs. L. about the Trinity.

....I see that I am still in the midst of telling you abt. Edw. & theology. Well, he asked Mrs. Lucas whether God was a man or not. She said, yes, then Edw. said, were there 2 Gods? So Mrs. L. had to admit that there were 3. tho' they were all one & the same really, the Father, the Son & the Holy Ghost. Edw. asked if the Holy Ghost was like God's Hand (v. close, isn't it?). Mrs. L. knew that if left at that, Edw. would think of a hand quite literally so said, Not quite: the Holy Ghost is God's Love. Edw. had not mentioned the subject again & probably would not do so for another fortnight; then, when everyone thought that he must have entirely forgotten, he would continue his enquiry, showing that he had been thinking deeply & constantly on the question ever since last it was discussed! Edw. can still walk thro' his father's legs but has to bend his head a little now.

15th Dec. Hoath, Kent. From JDH. My mother tells me that she was taking me down Bank St. in Ashford on a hot day & it was crowded with people shopping, & I asked loudly (I had a high penetrating voice) "Where did Aunty Denise's baby come from?" & my mother, having read that you should answer such questions the minute they are asked, replied "from inside Aunty Denise" (or something like that) & then I was silent & thoughtful for ages, & she was dreading the next question, because the last had made some people look, & then I said "Can I have an ice cream now?" Which shows the significant difference between me & Edw. Lucas.

On December 5 Charles de Gaulle (1890 – 1970), is re-elected as French president.

Churchill's quote: *Democracy is the worst form of government except all those other forms that have been tried.*

The northeast side of the Mount Washington Resort, Bretton Woods, New Hampshire, USA, where the United Nations Monetary and Financial Conference took place in July 1944.

392 BC. Plato is 36 years old.
A peace conference is held in Sparta, but it is unsuccessful.
Carthage attacks again Syracuse in Sicily, but it is defeated.
Isocrates (436 BC – 338 BC, the most influential Greek rhetorician, who amassed a considerable fortune) sets up a school of rhetoric in Chios (the 5th largest of the Greek islands, in the Aegean Sea, 7 km west of Anatolian coast, 200 km east of Athens). Because of Plato's attacks on the sophists, Isocrates' school — having its roots in rhetoric, the domain of the sophists — came to be viewed as unethical and deceitful. Yet many of Plato's criticisms are hard to substantiate in the actual work of Isocrates. At the end of Phaedrus, Plato even shows Socrates praising Isocrates. Isocrates saw the ideal orator as someone who must possess not only rhetorical gifts, but also a wide knowledge of philosophy, science, and the arts. He promoted the Greek ideals of freedom, self-control, and virtue. In this he influenced several Roman rhetoricians, such as Cicero (106

BC – 44 BC, Roman philosopher, politician and orator) and Quintilian (35 – 100, Roman rhetorician from Hispania), and influenced the core concepts of liberal arts education.
Cicero's quote: *Gratitude is not only the greatest of virtues, but the parent of all the others.*

1966 – Lucas publishes at Oxford *The Principles of Politics*, (second edition in 1985), where he develops his account of reasoning in the humanities, applying it to the life of political communities. Here, the relations of morality to law are well explored. This work contributed to the revival of political philosophy.

In October 1966 Lucas family moves to North Lodge, Rose Lane, Oxford, opposite Botanical Gardens, and near Magdalen Bridge.

On January 12, the United States President Lyndon Johnson (1908 – 1973) states that the United States should stay in South Vietnam until Communist aggression there is ended. On July 18, the manned spaceflight *Gemini X* (with John Young and Michael Collins) is launched. After docking with an unmanned spacecraft Agena target vehicle, the astronauts then set a world altitude record of 763 km.

Sweden stops working on nuclear weapons.

Darwin's quote: *It is not the strongest of the species that survive, nor the most intelligent, but the one most responsive to change.*

391 BC. Plato is 37 years old.
Persia fights against Sparta, and for control of Cyprus.
For the first time that a force of light infantry defeats a unit of Spartan hoplites (heavy infantry).
The Roman Republic is attacked by the Gauls (Celts).
Mozi, Chinese philosopher during the Hundred Schools of Thought period (early Warring States period (476 BC – 221 BC)), born c. 470 BC, dies. He founded the school of Mohism that argued strongly against Confucianism and Daoism. His philosophy emphasized self-restraint, self-reflection and authenticity, rather than obedience to ritual. During the Warring States period, Mohism

was actively developed and practiced in many states, but fell out of favor when the legalist Qin Dynasty (221 BC – 206 BC) came to power.

Plato's quote: *Let parents bequeath to their children not riches, but the spirit of reverence.*

1967 – Lucas is member of the Archbishops' Commission on Christian Doctrine, 1967-1976.

July 21st, Deborah Joan Lucas born, suffering from Down's Syndrome. For many years cared for at home, with help from the NHS. Then looked after by Sheila and Dave Wright, in Chard, Somerset, which greatly eased the burden on her parents. In spite of many operations in early life, and illnesses thereafter, Deborah is still alive and visits her parents once a month. She cannot talk, but can make her wishes known. She likes to walk round the village with her father.

The President of the British Academy is Sir Kenneth Clinton Wheare (1907 – 1979, President 1967 – 1971, Australian academic, Vice-Chancellor of the University of Oxford (1964 – 1966)).

On February 8 France launched its Diademe-C satellite and on February 15, its Diademe-D satellite into Earth orbit. These satellites were magnetically stabilized, which limited their tractability in the southern hemisphere.

Darwin's quote: *A man who dares to waste one hour of time has not discovered the value of life.*

390 BC. Plato is 38 years old, and he has his first journey to Sicily and Italy (early 390 BC to summer 388 BC). Now Plato has his first real attention to Pythagoreanism, which was undergoing a renaissance in South Italy, under the leadership of Archytas of Tarentum. First acquaintance with Dion of Syracuse (brother-in-law of Dionysius I), and with the young Dionysius II (who became tyrant in 367 BC on the death of his father). Plato departed to Aegina, on orders of Dionysius I.

On July 18 the Gauls attack Rome, but the Capitoline Hill is not captured. Marcus Furius Camillus (c 446 BC – 365 BC, Roman general and statesman, called Second Founder of Rome) appears with an army, ejects the Gauls from Rome, and then defeats them outside Rome.

Andocides, Athenian orator, logographer (speech writer) and politician, born in 440 BC, dies at 50.

Plato's quote: *Music is the movement of sound to reach the soul for the education of its virtue.*

1968 – Lucas writes on College life:
"Often it seems wrong to be enjoying the good things of College life. In America I could get at least twice as much for what I do, and academics are generally better paid in other countries than they are in Oxford. But still, I do live well, better than many of my fellow human beings; if not exactly arrayed in purple, I do fare sumptuously twice a day, and my lot is cast in an extremely pleasant place.

Is it wrong? Many say Yes, and wax indignant in Parliament or the columns of the press at the easy life I lead. In part, no doubt it is just envy, and in part muddled thinking. I cannot stop people being envious, but I am supposed to be able to clear up muddled thinking, so let me try that. In the first place there are arguments centered on me. It is bad from my point of view that I should have it so lush. Because I regularly over-eat, I shall get fatty deposits in the heart, and be brought down to an early grave by the cholesterol in my blood, and then discover, too late, that I have forfeited my soul's salvation, because I did not in my sojourn on earth remember Lazarus in Blackbird Ley. On the score of bodily health many of my elderly colleagues evidently feel themselves in danger. Now that fasting has gone out, dieting has come in, and the succulent stews provided by the chef at lunch are passed over in favour of rabbit food by the health-conscious. But what is good for a middle-aged don is not necessarily good for the younger man. The ethos of colleges is still that of the young male, who eats a lot and burns it up arguing or playing squash. Although individual fellows are wise to exercise restraint for their health's sake, there is no argument from health that we ought corporately to adopt a geriatric diet.

Perhaps, however, we should be morally better if we did. But there is no merit in third-party fasting. If an individual whole-heartedly embraces the ascetic life, he witnesses to his conviction that there are greater goods than the satisfaction of the fleshly appetites; and a similar corporate expression in a monastic community, is equally expressive. Colleges, although in many ways like monasteries, were not founded to manifest the ideals of poverty or obedience, nor has that become part of their present-day function. There is no evidence that plain living conduces to high thinking, and quite a lot, so far as undergraduates are concerned, of the opposite - that a College thinks on its stomach. We think it part of our collective duty to see that our undergraduates are well fed: no reason has been given for supposing that the same does not hold good of a College thinks on its stomach. We think it part of our collective duty to see that our undergraduates are well fed: no reason has been given for supposing that the same does not hold good of us too.

Other arguments are of a less first-personal kind. The money spent on crème brûlée could be better spent on a new computer, or a professor of educational sociology, or on slum clearance in the inner cities. But that is to assume that money is completely transferable, and it is not. Only at the margin is money able to be switched from one sort of expenditure to another. It is one of the great fallacies of social engineering to think that we can collectively redirect men's efforts to carry out whatever the planners deem to be in the public interest. We can easily stop college chefs trying to do their best. But the result of stopping people doing their best seldom results in better things being done elsewhere. It is a recipe for waste rather than urban renewal.

Perhaps we should not feel guilty at the good things we enjoy, but only grateful, and not think fruitlessly that we should not have it so good, but constructively on ways of enabling other people to have it good too."

On January 5 in Czechoslovakia, the Communist Party's Central Committee votes out Antonin Novotny (1904 – 1975) as First Secretary and replaces him with Alexander Dubcek (1921 – 1992). Novotny remains the country's president, but it is the beginning of what will be known as the Prague Spring – a reference to the blossoming of reforms called "socialism with a human face", until the Soviet invasion.

The government of North Korea requests that East Germany shares enough equipment and expertise in order for North Korea to build its own nuclear power plant. East Germany declines to engage in "wide-scale collaboration" on nuclear matters with North Korea, suggesting that the government from Pyongyang works directly with the Soviet Union to develop its nuclear program.

Darwin's quote: *I have called this principle, by which each slight variation, if useful, is preserved, by the term of Natural Selection.*

389 BC. Plato is 39 years old.
Sparta attacks and defeats Acarnania (west-central Greece, along the Ionian Sea).
Athens recaptures Byzantium, and collects tribute from many ships and islands.
In China, Wu Qi (440 BC – 381 BC) the Prime Minister of the State of Chu enacts many reforms, but he is assassinated in 381 BC.

Plato's quote: *No man should bring children into the world, who is unwilling to persevere to the end in their nature and education.*

1970 –Lucas publishes at Oxford *The Freedom of the Will*, in which he gives the fullest statement of his argument for the metaphysical belief in human freedom, and against mechanism and determinism.
Lucas also publishes at Oxford *The Concept of Probability*, where he defends objective probabilities and Bernoulli's Theorem in particular.

Prime Minister of the United Kingdom is Edward Heath (1916 – 2005, PM 1970 – 1974).
On February 11 Japan becomes the fourth country to launch a satellite into orbit. On September 28 Anwar Sadat (1918 – 1981) becomes the president of Egypt.
Solzhenitsyn, 52, in 1970, wins the Nobel Prize for Literature (before the publication of "Gulag"), but the Soviet state protests, preventing him from receiving the prize for years. His unpublished manuscripts begin leaking to the West, and Solzhenitsyn's literary fame grows.

Darwin's quote: *The very essence of instinct is that it's followed independently of reason.*

388 BC. Plato is 40 years old, and having left Athens on Socrates' death to visit Megara (30 km west of Athens), and possibly Egypt, travels to Syracuse (on the east coast of Sicily) at the invitation of Dionysius I's (432 BC – 367 BC) brother-in-law Dion (408 BC – 354 BC, a disciple of Plato).

Plato's quote: *The direction in which education starts a man will determine his future in life.*

387 BC. Plato is 41 years old and is forced by Dionysius I to leave Syracuse, after having exercised the right of free speech too broadly. Plato returns to Athens, and outside its walls he founds the Platonic Academy (387 BC – 83 BC, the first higher learning institution, for 304 years, it is dedicated to the Attic (Attica is a region in the southeast part of the Attica peninsula, with Athens and Piraeus) hero in Greek mythology, Academus), where he taught Aristotle (384 BC – 322 BC) from 367 BC (when Aristotle was 17) until 347 BC. Now starts the second period of Plato's literary activity, until 367 BC: *Meno, Symposium, Phaedrus, Cratylus, Phaedo, Parmenides, Euthydemus, Republic, Theatetus, and Menexenus.*

The Corinthian War ends with Sparta and Persia victorious.

Dionysius I of Syracuse becomes the chief power in Greek Southern Italy.

In Rome, Marcus Furius Camillus introduces the Capitoline Games (Ludi Capitolini) in honor of Jupiter Capitolinus, and in commemoration of Rome's Capitol not being captured by the Gauls.

Plato's quote: *The learning and knowledge that we have, is, at the most, but little compared with that of which we are ignorant.*

1971 - 1973 – Lucas, A.J.P. Kenny, H.C. Longuet-Higgins and C.H. Waddington give the Gifford Lectures.at Edinburgh. They publish the first set under the title ``The Nature of Mind" in 1972 and the second set under the title ``The Development of Mind" in 1973. . (Gifford Lectures were established by the will of Adam Lord

Gifford (1820 – 1887) at the University of Edinburgh (1582, in the capital of Scotland, 525 km northwest of London)

The President of the British Academy is Sir Denys Lionel Page (1908 – 1978, President 1971 – 1974, Professor of Greek at Cambridge University).

On July 26, 1971, as part of the Apollo program, the launch of Apollo 15 takes place in the US. On July 31 the Apollo 15 astronauts become the first to ride in a lunar rover, a day after landing on the surface of the Moon.

Darwin's quote: *To kill an error is as good a service as, and sometimes even better than, the establishing of a new truth or fact.*

386 BC. Plato is 42 years old.
Persia attacks Cyprus and Egypt, but they resist.
The Chinese city of Handan (400 km southwest of Beijing) is founded by the State of Zhao (403 BC – 222 BC, one of the seven major states during the Warring States period of ancient China).

Aristophanes, Greek playwright, born c. 456 BC, dies at 70.
Plato's quote: *There is no harm in repeating a good thing.*

1972 – Lucas, A.J.P. Kenny, H.C. Longuet-Higgins and C.H. Waddington publish at Edinburgh *The Nature of Mind*.

Lucas also publishes *Gifford Lectures*.

On January 5 the 37th President of the United States, Richard Nixon (1913 – 1994) orders the development of a space shuttle program. In October, the First International Conference on Computer Communications is held in Washington, D.C., and hosts the first public demonstration of ARPAnet, a precursor of the Internet.

Sweden closes all activities related to nuclear weapons.

Darwin's quote: *How paramount the future is to the present when one is surrounded by children.*

385 BC. Plato is 43 years old, and in his Academy he is teaching mathematics, astronomy, and other sciences, as well as philosophy. Philanthropists bear all costs; students pay no fees.

Democritus (c. 460 BC – c. 370 BC, influential pre-Socratic philosopher, mathematician and astronomer, who formulated an atomic theory of the universe, father of modern science) announces, when he is 75, that the Milky Way (Via Lactea, which includes the Solar System, about 27,000 light-years from the Galactic Center) is a concentration of many distant stars (200 - 400 billions). It seems that Plato did not understand and did not appreciate the much older Democritus.

Democritus' quote: *It is greed to do all the talking but not to want to listen at all.*

1973 – Lucas publishes *A Treatise on Time and Space*, which includes an argument from the concept of time to that of space. He introduces a transcendental derivation of the Lorenz Transformations, based on Red and Blue exchanging messages (in Russian and Greek respectively) from their respective frames of reference, which demonstrates how these can be derived from a minimal set of philosophical assumptions. Time is possible only if either there are things that change or there is the possibility of communication. But both change and communication require the concept of entities qualitatively identical but numerically distinct. Time is thus more fundamental than space, and according to Lucas is a prerequisite of consciousness, as space is not. Lucas proceeds to argue that if persons are to be possible, there must be both time, objects and space of a kind that would ideally have Euclidean properties, and then to consider why it is that space has to be three-dimensional and space-time 3+1-dimensional. He further argues that Augustine, Boethius and Aquinas were wrong to represent God as timeless. There is another theory of time and space presented in this author's (M. Dediu) books.

Lucas, A.J.P. Kenny, H.C. Longuet-Higgins and C.H. Waddington publish at Edinburgh *The Development of Mind.*

Lucas also published in *Philosophy* "'Because You Are A Woman'", a critique of feminism.

Whitehead's quote: *But you can catch yourself entertaining habitually certain ideas and setting others aside; and that, I think, is where our personal destinies are largely decided.*
Alfred North Whitehead, 1861 – 1947, English mathematician and philosopher

384 BC. Plato is 44 years old.

Lysias (c. 445 BC – c. 380 BC, has a statue, in the Gardens of Versailles, by Jean Dedieu (or de Dieu, 1646 – 1727, one of the ancestors of the author of this book)) the Athenian orator, on the occasion of the Olympiad (the first Olympic Games were in the summer of 776 BC in Olympia), rebukes the Greeks for allowing themselves to be dominated by the Syracusan tyrant Dionysius I and by the barbarian Persians.

The Greeks found the colony of Pharos at the site of today's Stari Grad on the island of Hvar, in the Adriatic Sea, 850 km northwest of Athens.

Aristotle, Greek philosopher, is born to Phaestis and Nichomachus (died in 322 BC, at 62).

Demosthenes, Greek statesman and orator, is born (died in 322 BC, at 62).

Plato's quote: *We ought to esteem it of the greatest importance, that the fictions, which children first hear, should be adapted in the most perfect manner to the promotion of virtue.*

1974 - The President of the British Academy is Sir Isaiah Berlin (1909 – 1997, President 1974 – 1978, Russo-British scholar, Professor of Social and Political Theory at the University of Oxford).

Prime Minister of the United Kingdom is again Harold Wilson (1916 – 1995, PM 1974 – 1976, FRS, resigned due to ill health).

On March 8, Charles de Gaulle Airport opens in Paris, France. On April, the world population reaches 4 billions of people, estimated by the United States Census Bureau.

Solzhenitsyn, 56, is labeled a traitor by the Soviet state-run newspaper "Pravda". He is stripped of his citizenship and deported to West Germany. Solzhenitsyn lives in Switzerland, then continues his exile in Cavendish, Vermont, USA (160 km northwest of Boston), where he completes "The Red Wheel," a series of novels about the formation of the modern Soviet Union.

Whitehead's quote: *Civilization advances by extending the number of important operations, which we can perform without thinking of them.*

383 BC. Plato is 45 years old.
Sparta changes the government of Thebes, capital of Boeotia, 55 km northwest of Athens.
Plato's quote: *To love rightly is to love what is orderly and beautiful in an educated and disciplined way.*

1975 – 1978 – Lucas is member of the Lichfield Commission on Divorce and Remarriage.
On August 1, 1975, the Helsinki Accords, Helsinki Final Act, or Helsinki Declaration was the first act of the Conference on Security and Co-operation in Europe held in Finlandia Hall of Helsinki, Finland, during July and August 1, 1975. Thirty-five states, including the USA, UK, Canada, and most European states except Albania, signed the declaration in an attempt to improve relations between the Communist bloc and the West. The Helsinki Accords, however, were not binding, as they did not have treaty status, but they had a positive impact for the people looking for freedom in the Communist bloc.
Whitehead's quote: *Civilizations can only be understood by those who are civilized.*

382 BC. Plato is 46 years old.
A Theban general and statesman flees to Athens and attempts to liberate Thebes from Spartan control.
Plato's quote: *Good people do not need laws to tell them to act responsibly, while bad people will find a way around the laws.*

1976 –.Lucas publishes *Freedom and Grace*, a collection of essays and lectures, which includes a nice resolution of the Augustine/Pelagius controversy. This resolution is developed in the ensuing papers, which stress that grace, like personal relationships, is granted by personal favor, and not by merit. In the paper 'Non Credo', the opening paragraphs begin (respectively) with 'I do not believe in phenomenalism or solipsism, materialism, determinism, irrationalism, emotivism, pragmatism, or subjectivism.' Objects of non-belief mentioned in the succeeding paragraphs include Marx, Freud, self-help or self-improvement, demythologising, and death as the end of everything.

Lucas also publishes (Harmondsworth) *Democracy and Participation*, where he combines a discerning critique of the British political system with general arguments. The lack of accountability of senior civil servants, also criticized here, remains to be rectified.

Prime Minister of the United Kingdom is James Callaghan (1912 – 2005, PM 1976 – 1979, the only politician in British history who has served in all four Great Offices of State (PM, Chancellor of the Exchequer, Foreign Secretary and Home Secretary, and the last armed forces veteran PM).

Whitehead's quote: *Common sense is genius in homespun.*

381 BC. Plato is 47 years old.

Persia attacks Cyprus, which becomes vassal of Persia.

Tusculum (30 km southeast of Rome, abandoned in 1191) is conquered by the Roman Republic, and becomes the first "municipium cum suffragio" (municipium with vote), and thenceforth the city continues to hold the rank of a municipium.

Plato's quote: *Justice in the life and conduct of the State is possible only as first it resides in the hearts and souls of the citizens.*

1978 – Lucas publishes *Butler's Philosophy of Religion Vindicated*

The President of the British Academy is Sir Kenneth James Dover (1920 – 2010, President 1978 – 1981, President of Corpus Christi College, Oxford).

On April 10 Volkswagen becomes the second (after Rolls-Royce) non-American automobile manufacturer to open a plant in the United States, commencing production of the Rabbit, the North American version of the Volkswagen Golf, at the Volkswagen Westmoreland Assembly Plant near New Stanton, Pennsylvania (the plant closes in 1992). On April 18 the U.S. Senate votes 68–32 to turn the Panama Canal over to Panamanian control on December 31, 1999.

Mill's quote: *Unquestionably, it is possible to do without happiness; it is done involuntarily by nineteen-twentieths of mankind.*

379 BC. Plato is 49 years old.
Theba eliminates the Spartan control.
Plato's quote: *Man never legislates, but destinies and accidents, happening in all sorts of ways, legislate in all sorts of ways.*

1979 - Lucas family moves to Postmasters' Hall, Merton Street, Oxford.

Postmasters' Hall, one of the oldest houses in Oxford, on Merton St. in early morning sunlight. For many years Lucas family lived here.

Prime Minister of the United Kingdom is Margaret Thatcher (1925 – 2013, PM 1979 – 1990, FRS, Falklands War, privatization of many industries, the end of the Cold War, the Gulf War).

Taiwan has important dealings, for three years, with President Ferdinand Marcos (1917 – 1989) of the Philippines and Prime Minister Mahathir Mohamad (born 1925) of Malaysia.

On February 7 the dwarf-planet Pluto (discovered by Clyde W. Tombaugh (1906 – 1997, American astronomer) on February 18, 1930; Pluto's surface is 3.3% of Earth, gravity 6.7% of Earth, temperature -230° C, distance from the Sun 6 billions of km (40 times farther than Earth), it has 5 satellites) enters a 20-year period inside the orbit of the 8th and farthest gaseous planet Neptune (discovered by Urbain Le Verrier (1811 – 1877, French mathematician) and Johann Galle (1812 – 1910, German astronomer; Neptune's distance to the Sun is 4.5 billions of km (30 times farther than Earth), surface 15 Earths, gravity 1.14 Earth, temperature -200° C, it has 14 satellites) on 23 September 1846), for the first time in 230 years.

<u>Clifford's quote:</u> *An atmosphere of beliefs and conceptions has been formed by the labors and struggles of our forefathers, which enables us to breathe amid the various and complex circumstances of our life.* William Kingdon Clifford, 1845 – 1879, English mathematician and philosopher.

Mrs. Joan Mary Lucas, the mother of J.R. Lucas.

378 BC. Plato is 50 years old.

Athens allies itself with Thebes, and forms the Second Athenian Empire (378 BC – 355 BC). The confederacy includes most of the Boeotian cities and some of the Ionian Islands.

Dionysius I of Syracuse is defeated in his third war with Carthage.

The Murus Servii Tullii (Servian Wall, named after the sixth Roman King Servius Tullius (King 575 BC – 535 BC), 10 m height, 3.6 m wide at its base, 11 km long, with 16 main gates) is constructed around Rome. This is the first fortification that the Romans build around their home city.

Plato's quote: *Not to help justice in its need would be an impiety.*

1980 – Lucas publishes at Oxford *On Justice,* in which Lucas criticizes both utilitarianism and Rawlsianism (here labeled a form of egalitarianism). He takes Rawls to task for pursuing a dialogue with the underdog but none with the 'overdog'. At the same time, advocates of laissez-faire are criticized for assuming that the success of the successful is in no way due to society.

In July Microsoft's Bill Gates (born 1955, he will become the wealthiest man on Earth between 1995 – present (2016, over $82 billions)) agrees to create an operating system for the new IBM Personal Computer. In September, David Bradley (born 1949, engineer) becomes one of the "original 12" engineers working on the project (under Don Estridge (1937 – 1985, electrical engineer)) and is responsible for the ROM BIOS code and for developing the Control-Alt-Delete command.

On November 12, as part of the Voyager program, the NASA space probe *Voyager I* makes its closest approach to Saturn (the sixth gas (mainly hydrogen) planet from the Sun, at 1.5 billions of km (10 times farther than Earth), the second largest after Jupiter, it has a large ring of small satellites, surface is 83.7 earths, density less than water, gravity about the same as Earth, temperature -139º C), when it flies within 124,000 km (about the diameter of Saturn) of the planet's cloud-tops, and sends the first high resolution images back to scientists on Earth.

Clifford's quote: *If a belief is not realized immediately in open deeds, it is stored up for the guidance of the future.*

377 BC. Plato is 51 years old.
Sparta attacks Thebes.

Plato's quote: *The highest reach of injustice is to be deemed just when you are not.*

1981 – Lucas gives lectures at the University of Dundee (1881, 60 km north of Edinburgh, 585 km northwest of London).

The President of the British Academy is The Reverend Owen Chadwick (1916 – 2015, President 1981 – 1985, British Anglican clergyman, Professor of History, Cambridge).

On March 5, the ZX81, a pioneering British home computer, is launched by Sinclair Research, going on to sell over 1.5 millions of units worldwide.

On April 3 the Osborne 1, the first successful portable computer, is unveiled at the West Coast Computer Faire in San Francisco, USA.

On August 12 the IBM Personal Computer is released.

Clifford's quote: *It is wrong always, everywhere, and for anyone, to believe anything upon insufficient evidence.*

376 BC. Plato is 52 years old.
Athens wins a naval victory over Sparta.
Olympias is born, future wife of King Philip II of Macedon (382 BC – 336 BC, King 359 BC – 336 BC), and mother of Alexander the Great (356 BC – 323 BC, 343 BC – 340 BC Aristotle is the tutor of Alexander, King 336 BC – 323 BC).

Plato's quote: *All the gold which is under or upon the Earth is not enough to give in exchange for virtue.*

1982 –Lucas' mother passes away.

1984 – Lucas publishes at Oxford *Space, Time and Causality,* where he presents a series of lectures on the philosophy of science.

Lucas also publishes in *Philosophy* 'The Alternative Sex', where he distinguishes feminism from femininity and explains that he remained prepared to defend pay differentials between male and female workers.

On January 10, under the 40th US President Ronald Reagan (1911 – 2004), the United States and the Vatican (Holy See) restore full diplomatic relations.

Clifford's quote: *No simplicity of mind, no obscurity of station, can escape the universal duty of questioning all that we believe.*

373 BC. Plato is 55 years old.
In 374 BC Aristotle is 10 and his father dies.
Athens wins a battle against Sparta.
The ancient Greek city of Helike (northern Peloponnese, 2 km from the Corinthian Gulf, near Boura, 150 km west of Athens) is destroyed by a massive earthquake and tsunami, in the winter.
The Temple of Apollo in Delphi (on the south-western spur of Mount Parnassus, in the valley of Phocis, 120 km northwest of Athens) is destroyed by the earthquake.
Plato's quote: *At the touch of love, everyone becomes a poet.*

J. R. Lucas on November 3, 2006, at the International Conference "John Stuart Mill, 1806 – 2006".

1985 - The President of the British Academy is Sir Randolph Quirk (born 1920, President 1985 – 1989, Professor of English language and literature at University College London, currently sits as a crossbencher in the House of Lords).
On January 1st the Internet's Domain Name System is created, and Greenland is withdrawn from the European Economic Community.

On January 21 the U.S. President Ronald Reagan is sworn in for a second term in office.

Clifford's quote: *Our lives are guided by that general conception of the course of things, which has been created by society for social purposes.*

372 BC. Plato is 56 years old.
Thessaly allies with Athens, and then with Macedon.
Mencius is born, future Chinese philosopher (died c. 289 BC).

Plato's quote: *Love is the joy of the good, the wonder of the wise, the amazement of the Gods.*

Reverend Egbert de Grey Lucas, the father of J. R. Lucas, drawing by Hermione Hammond.

A drawing of J.R. Lucas by Rob Mangles

1986 – Professor Mircea Eliade (1907 – 1986), well-known specialist in the history and philosophy of religion, University of Chicago, USA, passes away.

On January 1st Spain and Portugal enter the *European Community*, which later becomes the European Union.

On January 24 the Voyager 2 (launched on August 20, 1977, at Cape Canaveral LC-41, Florida, USA, and still working now (2016)) space probe makes its first encounter (at a distance of 81,500 km) with Uranus (the seventh gas (mostly hydrogen and helium) planet from the Sun, discovered with a telescope (for the first time in history) by William Herschel (1738 – 1822, German-born British astronomer and composer), in 1781, 2.9 billions of km from the Sun (19 times farther than Earth), its surface is 16 Earths, gravity 0.9 of Earth, temperature -200° C, it has 27 satellites).

Churchill's quote: *Mountaintops inspire leaders but valleys mature them.*

Mr. and Mrs. Lucas and their four children.

371 BC. Plato is 57 years old.

Thebes wins a battle at Leuctra against Sparta.

The city of Megalopolis is founded in Arcadia, center of Peloponnese, 150 km southwest of Athens.

It is suggested that Aristotle and Ephorus have observed the original comet associated with the Kreutz Sungrazers family of comets, which passes perihelion at this time.

Plato's quote: *Music is a moral law. It gives soul to the universe, wings to the mind, flight to the imagination, and charm and gaiety to life and to everything.*

The eldest grandson of J. R. Lucas – Johnny Lucas, around 2012.

1987 – Lucas gives lectures at Calvin College (1876) in Grand Rapids, Michigan, USA (220 km northeast of Chicago).

When Lucas was working on his invention, and had some business contacts for possible implementation of his invention, he wrote:

"I began to dream of Royalties. The original agreement with Isis Innovations gave me at first the lion's share of the Royalties after Isis Innovations expenses had been met, tapering off to about a quarter when they were reaching half a million pounds, with another quarter going to ``my department'' (in my case my College). My eyes and thoughts gravitated towards the upper end, and I arranged to see the Warden of Merton.

I wanted to make it possible for an undergraduate to come to university and not go down saddled with debt. Although many people would not be put off, and some indeed would regard it as a good investment leading to a larger income, others, particularly if they had a vocation to teach or to take Holy Orders, would have no realistic prospect of earning enough to pay off the debt, and would have it hanging over them for the rest of their lives. In order to attract good people, who might otherwise be put off, the money would have to be promised before the undergraduate came up, and would therefore need to be awarded at the time of the entrance exam.

A separate, competitive exam taken at about the same time was indicated. In what subjects? I told the Warden that I should like Mathematics and Greek, deliberately cutting across the great divide that has marked English education and damaged English culture.

Mathematics has the virtue of being very difficult, being essential for most other sciences, and best learned when young. Greek is also difficult, and is the language the first thinkers used to express their thoughts. It is pre-eminently the language of reason. Many of the political problems that beset us today were first encountered by the Greeks, and we can still learn what to do, and what not to do, by studying what they thought and did. The Warden was not so much skeptical as cautious. If we demanded Greek, we would restrict the candidates to the remaining three hundred good schools that still teach Greek. I was ready for that one. ``Not just classical Greek, but Hellenistic Greek as well, including New Testament Greek.

I envisaged candidates having to translate two out of four unseen: one from Plato, one from Xenophon, one from the New Testament and one from the Didache, or the Shepherd of Hermas, or the like. I imagined a mathematically inclined boy in Sunderland (where an old Mertonian was a parish priest). Around his sixteenth birthday his math's master talks about his university prospects, and mentions these Mertonian awards. ``But I don't know any Greek, Sir''. ``You don't now, but go along the Vicarage of St Luke's Pallion, knock on the door, and ask the Vicar if he can tell you where to buy a Greek testament with a good crib and vocab. He will almost certainly tell you, possibly lend you a copy of his own, and quite possibly offer to help you to get going''

It would be perfectly possible for him in two years to get up enough New Testament Greek to make a decent showing at translating some passages unseen. And if his math was good enough, he might win an award. If he did, he would have to make two undertakings: not to borrow money from any other source; and not to take paid employment in the vac. He would be free to read any final honour school that he could do so with profit. His fees would all be paid. He would have a living allowance enough for a moderate standard of living---not beer every night and Commem Balls, but enough to join the Union and play games. The exact details of financing I had not worked out---there might have to be nominal loans; but at the end of three or four years when he went down all loans would be cancelled, and he would start adult life debt-free.

It was an entrancing prospect. And I dreamt that I might extend it to my other Oxford college, Balliol, and to my Cambridge college, Corpus, and perhaps even further afield, Durham and York, each offering between four and seven awards each ear, if the points prospered.

But the dream faded."

The Chancellor of the University of Oxford is Roy Jenkins (1920 – 2003, Chancellor 1987 – 2003, President of the European Commission).

On January 8, the Dow Jones Industrial Average closes for the first time above 2,000, gaining 8.30 to close at 2,002.25 (after 29 years, in 2016, it is over 15,000).

Churchill's quote: *I am an optimist. It does not seem too much use being anything else.*

From left to right: Mrs. Lucas, Deborah, Richard, Mr. Lucas, Edward.

370 BC. Plato is 58 years old.

Sparta invades Arcadia, but Thebes liberates Arcadia, and the capital city of Megalopolis is completed.

The sculptor Praxiteles begins his active career in Athens. He was the first to sculpt the nude female form in a life-size statue.

Eudoxus of Cnidus (408 BC – 355 BC, Greek astronomer, mathematician, scholar and student of Plato) develops the method of exhaustion (using an inscribed sequence of polygons) for mathematically determining the area under a curve.

Marcus Valerius Corvus is born, future Roman hero (died c. 270 BC).

From left to right: Mr. Lucas, Daniel, Antonia, Helen, Helena

Theophrastus is born, future Greek philosopher, and the successor of Aristotle in the Peripatetic school (died c. 285 BC, at 85).

Democritus of Abdera, Greek philosopher, dies at 90 (born c. 460 BC)

Hippocrates of Cos, Greek physician, dies at 90 (born c. 460 BC).

Hippocrates' quote: *Make a habit of two things: to help; or at least to do no harm.*

1988 – **Lucas is elected to the Fellowship of the British Academy**, thus bringing his career into balance with Plato's.

Plato set up his Academy so that philosophers could together pursue truth. .Two millennia later the British Academy was founded so that scholars could meet and share their different understandings of the humanities (please see below more comments at the date July 18, 2013).

On January 2, the Soviet Union begins its program of economic restructuring (perestroika) with legislation initiated by Premier Mikhail Gorbachev (born 1931, he had begun minor restructuring in 1985).

Churchill's quote: *My most brilliant achievement was my ability to be able to persuade my wife to marry me.*

The eldest grandson of J. R. Lucas – Johnny Lucas

369 BC. Plato is 59 years old.
Thebes defeats Sparta and occupies some of its territory.
Athens allies with Sparta. Macedonia occupies Thessaly, but Thebes liberates Thessaly.

Zhuang Zhou is born, future Chinese Taoist philosopher (dies c. 286 BC).

Theaetetus, Athenian mathematician, dies at 48 (born c. 417 BC).

Plato's quote: *Poets utter great and wise things, which they do not themselves understand.*

1989 – Lucas publishes at Oxford *The Future: an Essay on God, Temporality and Truth*, in which the view that God is timeless is rejected as making him less than personal. By creating free, autonomous creatures, God freely limits his infallible omniscience. Lucas gives a detailed analysis of tenses and time, arguing that "the Block universe gives a deeply inadequate view of time. It fails to account for the passage of time, the pre-eminence of the present, the directedness of time and the difference between the future and the past" and in favor of a tree structure in which there is only one past or present (at any given point in space-time), but a large number of possible futures. "We are by our own decisions in the face of other men's actions and chance circumstances weaving the web of history on the loom of natural necessity". This work is well constructed to expound for students issues relating to the modal logic of knowledge and foreknowledge, and well explores the modal differences between past, present and future.

The elder son of J.R. Lucas – Edward (right), with the youngest granddaughter Isabel.

There were many controversies over the contents of political reform, but a commitment to reform served as a binding force for both Eastern Europe and China, right until the spring of 1989. Then, the same reform processes led to diametrically opposite political solutions, and turned into a source for difference and separation, because the Eastern Europe integrated into the democratic Western Europe, while China continued with its communist political system, changing only the economic system, in order to better compete with the US, Japan and Western Europe..

The President of the British Academy is Sir Anthony Kenny (born 1931, President 1989 – 1993, philosopher, Pro-Vice-Chancellor of the University of Oxford).

Churchill's quote: *Criticism may not be agreeable, but it is necessary. It fulfills the same function as pain in the human body. It calls attention to an unhealthy state of things.*

J. R. Lucas (right) and M. Dediu on November 3, 2006, at the International Conference "John Stuart Mill, 1806 – 2006".

368 BC. Plato is 60 years old, and his "Republic" is completed. It lays down the rules for an ideal, righteous society, and suggests that kings ought to be philosophers (or at least taught by philosophers).

Thebes controls Thessaly.

The King of Macedonia is assassinated.

Plato's quote: *Wise men speak because they have something to say; fools because they have to say something.*

1990 - Lucas and P.E. Hodgson publish at Oxford *Spacetime and Electromagnetism: An essay on the philosophy of the special theory of relativity,* in which he defends a realist interpretation of the Special Theory of Relativity. Unlike the past, the future is genuinely open

Prime Minister of the United Kingdom is John Major (born 1943, PM 1990 – 1997, Gulf War, privatization of British Rail).

On January 1st, 1990, Poland becomes the first country in Eastern Europe to begin abolishing its state socialist economy. Poland also withdraws from the Warsaw Pact.

Churchill's quote: *To improve is to change; to be perfect is to change often.*

Lucas relaxing in the Sun.

367 BC. Plato is 61 years old, and goes for the second time to Syracuse.
Thebes invades Peloponnesus, then withdraws.
Sparta wins a battle with Arcadia.

Dionysius I of Syracuse (c 432 BC – 367 BC) dies at 65, and is succeeded as tyrant of the city by his son Dionysius II (c 397 BC – 343 BC). As the younger Dionysius (30 years old) is weak and inexperienced, Dion (408 BC – 354 BC), brother-in-law of the elder Dionysius, assumes control and persuades Plato, whose friendship he has acquired, to train the new tyrant in the practical application of his philosophical principles.

The temple to Concordia (the goddess who embodies agreement and harmony in marriage and society), on the Forum Romanum (a rectangular forum (plaza) in the center of the city, from 750 BC) in Rome is built by Marcus Furius Camillus (c 446 BC – 365 BC).

The Greek from Macedon philosopher and scientist, Aristotle (384 BC – 322 BC), at 17, is sent to Athens as a pupil at Plato's Academy where he studies rhetoric. Aristotle writes about Plato after his death.

Plato's quote: *Astronomy compels the soul to look upwards and leads us from this world to another.*

1991 – 1993 – Lucas is President of the British Society for the Philosophy of Science (started in 1948 as a Group, and in 1959 was established).

In February 1991 Russia has an ambiguous policy towards North Korea, and this fact facilitates the first North Korean nuclear crisis.

Churchill's quote: *My rule of life, prescribed as an absolutely sacred rite, smoking cigars, and also the drinking of alcohol before, after and, if need be, during all meals, and in the intervals between them.*

366 BC. Plato is 62 years old and leaves Syracuse.

Athens founds the town of Kos, on the island of Kos, in the Aegean Sea, 300 km southeast of Athens.

Thebes makes peace with Sparta, and then turns its attention on Athens, which is trying to revive its maritime empire, and is interfering in Macedonian dynastic quarrels.

Dion (brother-in-law of Dionysius I) asked Plato to educate the new ruler of Syracuse, Dionysius II, in the practical application of Plato's philosophical principles, but Dionysius II does not want, and Dion and Plato are banished from Syracuse.

Plato's quote: *We ought to fly away from Earth to heaven as quickly as we can; and to fly away is to become like God, as far as this is possible; and to become like him is to become holy, just, and wise.*

1992 – On January 1st, the 41st President George H. W. Bush (born 1924) becomes the first U.S. President to address the Australian Parliament.

On January 2nd, the first President of Russia, Boris Yeltsin (1931 – 2007) ends price controls, resulting in prices of some goods and services becoming 3 to 5 times more expensive. This in effect ends the command economy in Russia.

Churchill's quote: *My wife and I tried two or three times in the last 40 years to have breakfast together, but it was so disagreeable we had to stop.*

365 BC. Plato is 63 years old, and from now until 361 BC works on and publishes The *Sophistes* and the *Politicus.*

Athens wins against Persia at Samos.

Antisthenes, Athenian philosopher, born. c. 445 BC, dies at 80.

Plato's quote: *A state arises, as I conceive, out of the needs of mankind; no one is self-sufficing, but all of us have many wants.*

1993 – Lucas publishes at Oxford *Responsibility,* in which he supplies a synoptic view of a broad field of topics (punishment, reward, desert, free will, rationality, consequentialism, political accountability, business ethics and the Atonement) unified through their links with responsibility, understood here as answerability. The work concludes with Lucas's 'Which? Guide to Theories of Punishment' (280-285). Five theories are depicted (three utilitarian and two retributivist), together with their merits, demerits, advocates and critics.'

Lucas' Gödelian argument is strengthened by the observation that sufficiently complex analogue recurrent neural networks were not equivalent to Turing Machines.

The President of the British Academy is Sir Keith Thomas (born 1933, President 1993 – 1997, Professor of Modern History in the University of Oxford).

Churchill's quote: *I have taken more out of alcohol than alcohol has taken out of me.*

<u>**364 BC**</u>. Plato is 64 years old.
Thebes builds a strong fleet, and wins a battle against Thessaly.
Arcadia wins a battle against Sparta.
The Chinese astronomer Gan De from the State of Qi reportedly discovers the moon Ganymede, belonging to Jupiter, and makes the earliest known sunspot observations.

Plato's quote: *Courage is knowing what not to fear.*

<u>**1996**</u> – Lucas retires, and moves to Lambrook House, East Lambrook, Somerset

Lucas and M.R. Griffiths (1972 – 2016) publish (Basingstoke) *Ethical Economics,* in which he argues that business-people have responsibilities beyond those of making profits for themselves or for shareholders, responsibilities to customers, community and environment, grounded in the co-operative nature of business. At the same time a skeptical view is taken of the possibilities for full employment, for socialism, or for distributive justice ever becoming the basis of an economy, a limited scope is assigned to socially responsible investment, and a rather benevolent view is taken of downsizing and of the 'trickle-down effect'.

Lucas publishes 'The Temporality of God' in Robert John Randall, Nancey Murphy and C. J. Isham (eds.), *Quantum Cosmology and the Laws of Nature: Scientific Perspectives on Divine Action*, (2nd edn.) Vatican City State and Berkeley, California. If God is temporal, God's time-frame has priority over all others. God's ability to hear our prayers and answer them is held to require temporal but omniscient knowledge, held simultaneously both with human prayers and with all other events occurring throughout the universe at the same time as they are offered.

Churchill's quote: *I have never developed indigestion from eating my words.*

361 BC. Plato is 67 years old, and returns once more to Syracuse to teach the young Syracusan tyrant Dionysius II. He fails to reconcile the tyrant to Dion, who Dionysius II banished in 366 BC. Because of this, Plato is forced to flee Syracuse, to save his life. This third journey to Sicily was on the invitation of Dion. Plato is forced to live outside the palace, at the camp of the mercenaries. Dion wants revolution, but Plato refused to participate. With the intervention of Archytas of Tarentum, Plato is allowed to return to Athens (summer, 360 BC).

Thebes lost its power.

Plato's quote: *Democracy passes into despotism.*

1997 –The President of the British Academy is Sir Tony Wrigley (born 1931, President 1997 – 2001, historical demographer, Master of Corpus Christi College, Cambridge).

Prime Minister of the United Kingdom is Tony Blair (born 1953, PM 1997 – 2007, Hong Kong handover, independence for the Bank of England, Minimum wage introduced, 1999 NATO bombing of Yugoslavia, War in Afghanistan and Iraq).

In March Lucas and his wife go to Libya to see total eclipse of the Sun.

Franklin's quote: *Fatigue is the best pillow.* Benjamin Franklin, 1706 – 1790, one of the Founding Fathers of the USA, author, scientist.

360 BC. Plato is 68 years old, and writes the dialogues *Timaeus* and *Kritias*, first mentioning Atlantis. Between now and 348 BC is the last period of Plato's literary activity: *Philebus, Letter 7, The Laws*.

Egypt has a new king with the help from Sparta.

Sparta has a new king.

The Gauls again reach the gates of Rome, but are beaten back.

Pyrrho of Elis (city in northwest Peloponnesus, on the Ionian Sea) is born, Greek skeptic philosopher (died c. 270 BC, at 90).

Plato's quote: *Democracy... is a charming form of government, full of variety and disorder; and dispensing a sort of equality to equals and unequals alike.*

Mrs. Lucas at Leptis Magna in March 1997.

2000 – On October 15th Lucas publishes *The Conceptual Roots of Mathematics*, in which he argues for a qualified logicism. Mathematical arguments are not all deductive, and are best thought of as a dialogue, yet mathematical concepts remain grounded in logic. In a further *Which?* guide, this time to geometry, Euclid's is recommended as the Best Buy, as was previously argued, on different grounds, in *A Treatise on Space and Time*. Lucas writes: "My chief claims are that mathematics is as much a doing as a seeing, and that if we think of mathematical argument as a dialogue between two people, instead of a monologue, we get a much better understanding of mathematical proof. The simplest example is ``Mathematical Induction" or Argument by Recursion, as I call it. Mathematics is based on logic, but cannot be reduced to it. This follows from Gödel's Theorem." Lucas explained Gödel's Theorem in a book, but it is very difficult. In his book, he says that it is the *pons asinorum* (bridge of asses = something difficult to understand) of modern mathematics.

Mr. and Mrs. Lucas on November 3, 2006, at the International Conference "John Stuart Mill, 1806 – 2006".

Franklin's quote: *Be slow in choosing a friend, slower in changing.*

J. R. Lucas (right) and M. Dediu on November 3, 2006, at the International Conference "John Stuart Mill, 1806 – 2006".

357 BC. Plato is 71 years old.

Between 367 BC and 347 BC, when Aristotle was at the Academy, age 17 to 37, he wrote two works: "Topics" and "Sophistical Refutations". "Topics" talks about how to construct arguments for a position one has already decided to adopt. His other work, "Sophistical Refutations" talks about how to detect weaknesses in the arguments of others.

The Athens' island Rhodes falls to Persia.

King Phillip II of Macedon (382 BC – 336 BC, King 359 BC – 336 BC), having disposed of an Illyrian threat, occupies the Athenian city of Amphipolis (which commands the gold mines of Mount Pangaion). Philip II now has control of the strategic city which secures the eastern frontier of Macedonia and gives him access into Thrace.

Philip II of Macedon marries Olympias, the Molossian princess of Epirus, thus helping to stabilize Macedonia's western frontier.

In Syracuse, the brother-in-law of Dionysius I, Dion (408 BC – 354 BC), exiled from Syracuse in 366 BC by Dionysius II, assembles a force of 1,500 mercenaries at Zacynthus and sails to Sicily. Dion takes power from the weak Dionysius II, who is exiled and flees to Locri.

Plato's quote: *Dictatorship naturally arises out of democracy, and the most aggravated form of tyranny and slavery out of the most extreme liberty.*

2001 – The President of the British Academy is The Viscount Runciman of Doxford (born 1934, President 2001 – 2005, historical sociologist, Senior Research Fellow at Trinity College, Cambridge).

On January 20 George W. Bush (born 1946) is sworn into office as President of the United States.

Franklin's quote: *Remember not only to say the right thing in the right place, but, far more difficult still, to leave unsaid the wrong thing at the tempting moment.*

356 BC. Plato is 72 years old.
Phillip II of Macedon captures more cities from Athens.
The holy temple of Delphi is destroyed in the Sacred War.
A plebeian is chosen for the first time as a dictator in Rome.
On July 20 is born Alexander the Great, future King of Macedonia (died 323 BC, at 32).

Alexander's quote: *I am indebted to my father for living, but to my teacher for living well.*

2002 – Lucas publishes "The Gödelian Argument" in The Truth Journal.

In May – at Potter's Bar (Hertfordshire, 29 km north of London), there is a train crash.

On February 19, NASA's *2001 Mars Odyssey* space probe begins to map the surface of Mars, using its thermal emission imaging system.

Lucas relaxing at a meeting.

Franklin's quote: *Your net worth to the world is usually determined by what remains after your bad habits are subtracted from your good ones.*

355 BC. Plato is 73 years old.

Persia forces Athens to conclude a peace with many losses.

Xenophon, Greek historian, soldier, mercenary and an admirer of Socrates, born. c. 431 BC, dies at 76.

Eudoxus of Cnidus, Greek astronomer and mathematician, born c. 408 BC, dies at 53.

Plato's quote: *Excess generally causes reaction, and produces a change in the opposite direction, whether it be in the seasons, or in individuals, or in governments.*

2003 – Lucas and Basil Mitchell publish (Ashgate) *An Engagement with Plato's Republic*, which adds to the literature on this essential work, as commentary, but more as critical guide and companion. Lucas writes: "It is not a standard commentary. Rather, it is a deliberately anachronistic attempt to make Plato accessible to the modern reader, and to engage him in dialogue with modern problems.

It was published on September 5th. It should have come out much earlier, but most unfortunately there was a muddle over the book-jacket, which was to be an adaptation of Raphael's School of Athens showing Plato talking with his pupils, some of them altered to be in modern dress and using a word-processor. Owing to a breakdown in communication, an uncorrected proof was used, with Plato more or less eclipsed by `Basil Mitchell' and `J.R. Lucas'. This was not the message we wish to convey. A new book-jacket has been printed, both for the hard-back and for the paper-back editions. If you buy the paper-back, make sure you have the correct outside, with us deferentially down in the right hand corner, taking our place among Plato's pupils, not lording it over them."

A public re-enactment of the Huxley-Wilberforce debate, which Lucas staged at a British Academy event in Kensington. Lucas writes: "On November 6th, 2003, I stood in for Bishop Wilberforce at the British Academy, at 5.15 pm, saying what he might have said now, with the benefit of 143 years hindsight."

The current Chancellor of the University of Oxford is Chris Patten (born 1944, Chancellor from 2003, former governor of Hong Kong and the BBC Trust).

Washington's quote: *Happiness and moral duty are inseparably connected.* George Washington, 1732 – 1799, one of the Founding Fathers and the first President of the USA (1789 – 1797).

354 BC. Plato is 74 years old.

In Syracuse, the tyrant Dion is assassinated.

Phillip II of Macedon takes a town from Athens, but loses an eye.

Rome defeats the Etruscans of the city of Caere.

Plato's quote: *Good actions give strength to ourselves and inspire good actions in others.*

2005 *Dictionary of Twentieth-Century British Philosophers* (2 vols.), ed. Stuart Brown, Bristol: Thoemmes Continuum, 2005, vol. I, 586-90; ISBN 1-84371-096-X

The President of the British Academy is The Baroness O'Neill of Bengarve (born 1941, President 2005 – 2009, politician and philosopher, Principal of Newham College, Cambridge).

On January 5, Eris, the largest known dwarf planet in the Solar System, is identified by a team led by Michael E. Brown (born 1965, American astronomer) using images originally taken on October 21, 2003, at the Palomar Observatory.

On January 14, the Huygens probe lands on Titan, the largest moon of Saturn.

Washington's quote: *Associate with men of good quality*

2006 J. R. Lucas is invited at the International Conference "John Stuart Mill, 1806 – 2006".

J. R. Lucas (right) and M. Dediu on November 3, 2006, at the International Conference "John Stuart Mill, 1806 – 2006", Faculty of Philosophy, University of Bucharest, Romania, celebrating two hundred years from the birth (on May 20, 1806, in Pentonville, on the northern border of Central London, United Kingdom) of John Stuart Mill.

351 BC. Plato is 77 years old.
Phoenicia (on the east cost of the Mediterranean Sea) and Cyprus revolt against Persia.
Demosthenes (384 BC – 322 BC, statesman and orator) tries to get the Athenians to cease depending on paid mercenaries, and return to the old concept of a citizen army. He also delivers his first Philippic, warning Athenians of the folly of believing that Philip's ill health will save Athens from the Macedonians. In response, Athens' citizens votes for increased armaments.
The Etruscans are badly defeated by the Romans, and abandon their attacks on the city and sue for peace.
First use of the heavy throwing spear, the pilum, in battle against the Gauls.
The first Roman plebeian is elected to the office of censor.
Plato's quote: *Only the dead have seen the end of war.*

2007 - Prime Minister of the United Kingdom is Gordon Brown (born 1951, PM 2007 – 2010, several banks nationalized, last PM to choose the date of a General Election).
On January 1st, Romania and Bulgaria join the European Union.
On June 8, the Space Shuttle Atlantis begins its mission.
Washington's quote: *Friendship is a plant of slow growth and must undergo and withstand the shocks of adversity before it is entitled to the appellation.*

350 BC. Plato is 78 years old, and proposes a geocentric model of the universe, with the stars rotating on a fixed celestial sphere.
Phillip II of Macedon wins against Epirus and Thrace.
The Gauls, once more threatening Rome, are decisively beaten by an army comprising Rome and its allies.

Aristotle argues for a spherical Earth, using lunar eclipses and other observations. Also he discusses logical reasoning in Organon (the standard collection of Aristotle's six works on logic. The name Organon was given by Aristotle's followers, the Peripatetics).

Praxiteles makes his most famous statue "Aphrodite of Knidos".

Dicaearchus is born, future Greek philosopher, cartographer, geographer, mathematician and polygraph (died c. 285 BC).

Shen Dao is born, future Chinese philosopher, known for his blend of Legalism and Taoism (died c. 275 BC).

Plato's quote: *Our object in the construction of the state is the greatest happiness of the whole, and not that of any one class.*

2008 – Lucas started suggesting that since Fellows are elected on the strength of their published work, the Academy ought to make available to any enquirer a list of each Fellow's published work.

2009 – The President of the British Academy is Sir Adam Roberts (born 1940, President 2009 – 2013, Emeritus Professor of International Relations at Oxford University).

2009 was the International Year of Astronomy.

On February 10, a Russian and an American satellite collide over Siberia, creating a large amount of space debris.

Washington's quote: *Government is not reason; it is not eloquent; it is force. Like fire, it is a dangerous servant and a fearful master.*

348 BC. Plato is 80 years old.

Persia takes Sidon.

Phillip II of Macedon conquers several cities from Athens.

Rome and Carthage make a trade agreement under which Carthage will not attack those Latin states which are faithful to Rome, which is now the dominant power in the Latin League.

Plato's quote: *The measure of a man is what he does with power.*

2010 Current Prime Minister of the United Kingdom is David Cameron (born 1966, PM from 2010, Libya intervention, London 2012 Summer Olympics, privatization of the Royal Mail, Iraq and Syria intervention).

In February NASA's Solar Dynamics Observatory (SDO) is launched, and the SDO uses various wavelengths to observe the Sun.

Washington's quote: *I hope I shall possess firmness and virtue enough to maintain what I consider the most enviable of all titles, the character of an honest man.*

347 BC. Plato passes away at 81, and his nephew Speusippus (c 408 BC – 338 BC, his mother Potone was Plato's sister, he developed the philosophy of Plato, but rejected the Theory of Forms), 61 years old, is named as head of the Academy.

The Athenian leader, Eubulus (c 405 BC – c 335 BC), works for peace with Philip II of Macedon (382 BC – 336 BC, King 359 BC – 336 BC). Demosthenes (384 BC – 322 BC) is among those who support a compromise. An Athenian delegation, comprising Demosthenes, Aeschines and Philocrates, is officially sent to Pella (capital of the kingdom of Macedon, 320 km northwest of Athens, 35 km northwest of Thessaloniki) to negotiate a peace treaty with Philip II.

Coinage is introduced into Rome for the first time.

Aristotle (384 BC – 322 BC, born in Stagira (275 km north of Athens, in central Macedonia, near the eastern coast of the Chalkidice peninsula, student of Plato for 20 years, from 367 BC (when Aristotle was 17) until 347 BC), now 37, leaves Athens due to the anti-Macedonian feeling that arises in Athens after Philip II of Macedon has sacked the Greek city-state of Olynthus (50 km southwest of Stagira) in 348 BC. With him goes another Academy member of note, Xenocrates (396 BC – 314 BC, Greek philosopher, mathematician, and leader (scholarch) of the Platonic Academy from 339 to 314 BC) of Chalcedon (ancient maritime town of Bithynia, in Asia Minor. It was located almost directly opposite Byzantium). They establish a new academy on the Asia Minor side of the Aegean Sea, at the newly built town of Assus (280 km northeast of Athens), where he was welcomed by King Hermias, and opened an Academy in this city. Aristotle also married Pythias, the adopted daughter of Hermias. In the Academy of Assus, Aristotle became a chief to a group of philosophers, and he made observations on zoology and biology. Aristotle and his wife move, in 344 BC, to Mytilene (the capital of the island of Lesbos, 30 km southwest of Assus) where he spends two years studying natural history and marine biology When the Persians attacked Assus, King Hermias was caught and put to death in 345 BC. Aristotle fled to Pella, the capital of Macedonia, in 343 BC, which was ruled by his friend King Philip II of Macedon. There, he tutored Philip's son, Alexander the Great (he was 13 to 16), for three years, between 343 BC and 340 BC.

Eudoxus of Cnidus (town in south-western Asia Minor, 330 km southeast of Athens), Greek philosopher, mathematician and astronomer, who has expanded on Plato's ideas, born 410 BC, dies at 63. Craters on Mars and the Moon are named in his honor. An algebraic curve (the Kampyle of Eudoxus) is also named after him.

Aristotle's quote: *It is the mark of an educated mind to rest satisfied with the degree of precision, which the nature of the subject admits, and not to seek exactness where only an approximation is possible.*

2012 – November 28, Lucas presses Professor Vicki Bruce for action on bibliographies, which need to be easily accessible to any enquirer.

2013 – On January 24th Lucas writes to T.J. Sutton, Esq
"Dear Tim,
What first alerted me was a year and half ago, when I was in Winchester for a special do, and was in Winchester Cathedral the previous day, where there was an exhibition to mark the four hundredth anniversary of the Authorised Version. Naturally, it was mostly about that, but in the North Choir Aisle there was an exhibition of other translations, all of the beginning of St John's Gospel. In one of them it said ``the Word became flesh". I suddenly realised that this was right, and that `was made' was a mistranslation, which after a few moments' thought I put down to the Latin fio being a semi-deponent verb, and having as its past tense factus sum. The Authorised Version had followed earlier translations where possible, and had therefore been influenced at this point by the Latin of the Vulgate, rather than the original Greek. I marveled that for

over seventy Christmases I had heard the Christmas gospel, and then gone on to sing the creed's `begotten, not made" without noticing the contradiction.

As I read St John's gospel, I was drawn to the highly heretical conclusion that it was written by St John (and not by another person of the same name, as some scholars claim). It was also originally written much earlier, (ca. 50 AD) than is commonly supposed, but went through several revisions, with a Postscript being added to a later one, and the text we have is, except for the last two verses, based on a disciple's own student text, with his marginal notes not rubbed out, and his own testimonial in the last two verses to the truthfulness of the author and the authenticity of the text.

A key piece of information came from the present Pope. He cited some evidence produced by some French scholars that suggested that Zebedee might have been as Lay Canon, as it were, who did a turn of being ``in residence" at the Temple. The Zebedees were not humble fisher folk, as I had always assumed, but prosperous members of the Fishmongers' Livery Guild (like the Merchant Tailors today). This was a key bit of the jigsaw, and made everything fit together. Sometime later I was explaining this to a neighbouring clergyman; he was not impressed, when I cited the Bishop of Rome as my fellow heretic. ``But is he qualified to have an opinion", he countered. I probed, and it then came out ``Had Cardinal Ratzinger read theology at Cambridge?". This gave me the answer to one remaining problem. In Acts, after St Peter and St John had given a very good account of the good news the Jewish establishment pooh-poohed them, saying that they were unlettered laymen. The Authorised version renders this as ``unlearned and ignorant men"; but the Greek need not mean that, but rather ``laymen with no letters after their name"---not been to Cambridge.

There is one question where your better knowledge of Greek would be a help. At 19:27b is the plural idia; I translate it `quarters' suggesting a somewhat commodious dwelling place; but does the plural imply that? It could mean `rooms'. The AV translates it by the singular `dwelling place'. St John would have been in his early twenties at the time of the crucifixion, Mrs. Zebedee would have been keeping her distance after her sons' venture had come unstuck. St John's having his own place hints at some degree of affluence, and I wonder whether the plural corroborates this. "

25 February 2013 - Lucas reports not being able, as an outside enquirer, to find the bibliography of a named Fellow.

Lucas raises question of why the British Academy does not, like the Royal Society, describe itself as a Learned Society.

10 May 2013 - Vicki Bruce breaks off discussion, saying ``On its website the Royal Society describes itself as "a Fellowship of the world's most eminent scientists and the oldest scientific academy in continuous existence". While in many of its activities the British Academy does have the character of a Learned Society, this by itself does not adequately capture the range of roles which it has (a further three roles, in addition to 'learned society' are set in the Strategic Framework).

I think little can be gained by continuing these email exchanges. The Academy has sought, in good faith, to address the points you have made and will continue to do so. We have changed the wording on the main home page, expanded the information on the Fellowship home page to make specific reference to published work being the basis for Fellows' election, introduced a system for holding bibliographies as part of Fellows' web entries and looked at ways to improve our search engine (already much improved but, as we all know, no search engine is ever perfect).

Robin will be emailing all Fellows next week to reinforce our shared desire for the website to carry more information, including bibliographies, on all Fellows. We have given these matters considerable priority and will of course keep you in touch with developments.

15 July 2013 - from Professor Graham Davies I thought I might ask a question under the Strategic Plan item, about why the Council has dropped 'learned society' from the Academy's roles there - do they no longer believe the Academy is a learned society, or do they believe it but not want to say it? That might be enough from me, as it bears directly on one of the points of your motion.

17 July 2013 - Intense heat in London causes many Fellows not to attend Annual General Meeting.

18 July 2013 - Lucas fails to persuade British Academy to describe itself as a Learned Society.

The current President of the British Academy is The Lord Stern of Brentford (born 1946, President from 2013, Professor of Economics and Government at the London School of Economics).

On February 21, American scientists use additive manufacturing to create a living lab-grown ear from collagen and animal ear cell cultures. In the future, it is hoped, similar ears could be grown to order as transplants for human patients suffering from ear trauma or amputation.

Washington's quote: *If we desire to avoid insult, we must be able to repel it; if we desire to secure peace, one of the most powerful instruments of our rising prosperity, it must be known, that we are at all times ready for War.*

344 BC. One year before, in 345 BC: King Hermias is killed by Persians.

Aristotle is 40 years old, and he travels from Assus 30 km south to Mytilene, the capital of the island of Lesbos, to study natural history, especially marine biology.

The Athenian statesman Demosthenes travels to Peloponnesus, in order to keep the local cities out of the Macedon's influence, but he is unsuccessful. Demosthenes then delivers the Second Philippic, which is a vehement attack against Philip II of Macedon.

An army from Corinth (80 km west of Athens) goes to Sicily (700 km west of Corinth), occupies Syracuse, and its tyrant Dionysius II goes in exile again.

Aristotle's quote: *Teaching is the highest form of understanding.*

2014

On January 1, Latvia officially adopts the euro as its currency and becomes the 18th member of the Eurozone.

Washington's quote: *Someday, following the example of the United States of America, there will be a United States of Europe.*

343 BC. Aristotle is 41 years old, and he tutors young Alexander, 13, in Pella, the capital of Macedonia, for three years.

The King of Persia Artaxerxes III (c 425 BC – 338 BC, King 358 BC – 338 BC) leads the Persian forces invading Egypt. Pharaoh Nectanebo II (360 BC – 342 BC) is forced to retreat to Memphis (20 km south of Giza). Then Nectanebo II leaves for exile in Nubia (south of Egypt). His departure marks the end of the 30th Dynasty, the last native house to rule Egypt. Egypt once again is reduced to a satrapy of the Persian Empire. A Persian satrap is put in place in Egypt. The walls of the country's cities are destroyed and its temples are plundered.

King Philip II of Macedon again marches against Cersobleptes, King of Thrace, defeats him in several battles, and reduces him to a tributary.

The native Italian tribes, the Lucanians and Bruttians, press down upon the Greek colonies of Magna Graecia, including Tarentum (southeast of Italy, 250 km east of Napoli). Responding to calls for help from these former Greek colonies, King Archidamus III (360 BC – 338 BC) of Sparta sets sail with a band of mercenaries for Italy.

The most powerful group of the native tribes in highland Italy, the confederated Samnites, swarm down into Campania (south of Rome, around Napoli). The city of Capua (25 km north of Napoli, 160 km southeast of Rome) appeals to Rome for help. The Romans respond, which begins the First Samnite War.

Aristotle's quote: *It is the mark of an educated mind to be able to entertain a thought without accepting it.*

2015 - Robin Attfield, 'Lucas, John Randolph', in *Cambridge Dictionary of Philosophy*, third edition, New York: Cambridge University Press, 2015, pp. 614-15

In November, Lucas was told by Mr. Andrew McNaughton that there was no sign of his invention having been used in the recently constructed new lines in China.

On January 1, Lithuania officially adopts the euro as its currency, replacing the litas, and becomes the nineteenth Eurozone country.

On January 15, the Swiss National Bank abandons the cap on the franc's value relative to the euro.

On March 6, NASA's multi-target orbiter *Dawn* (launched in 2007) enters orbit around Ceres (discovered by Giuseppe Piazzi (1746 – 1826, Italian astronomer) in Palermo, in 1801, is the largest object in the asteroid belt, which lies between the orbits of Mars and Jupiter, 950 km diameter), becoming the first spacecraft to visit a dwarf planet.

Washington's quote: *The basis of our political system is the right of the people to make and to alter their constitutions of government.*

342 BC. Aristotle is 42 years old, he is the guest of the King Philip II (40 years old) of Macedon, in his capital at Pella, and Aristotle tutors his son, Alexander, now 14 year old.

Philip II begins a series of campaigns in Thrace, to annex it to Macedonia. When the Macedonian army approaches Thracian Chersonese (the Gallipoli Peninsula), the Athenian general Diopeithes ravages this district of Thrace, thus inciting Philip's rage. Philip demands his recall. In response, the Athenian Assembly is convened. Demosthenes convinces the Athenians not to recall Diopeithes.

The Battle at the foot of Mount Gaurus (10 km west of Napoli), near Cumae, is a victory for the Romans, led by Marcus Valerius Corvus, over the Samnites.

In the course of the Warring States period, the state of Qi defeats the state of Wei in the Battle of Maling. This battle uses the military strategy of the general Sun Bin (descendent of Sun Tzu), and is the first battle in recorded history to give a reliable account of the handheld crossbow with trigger mechanism.

Aristotle's quote: *Nature does nothing uselessly.*

2016 –
Navy moves forward on common missile compartment for future U.S. and U.K. nuclear submarine. U.S. Navy strategic defense experts are moving forward on a long-term project to design a future ballistic missile nuclear submarine for the U.S. and United Kingdom.

Global demand for missiles and missile-defense systems will grow by more than 50 percent over the next decade, driven by the increasing threat of radical states and organizations with access to weapons of mass destruction, experts say.

Special Forces are testing personal drones, tiny stealth spy craft, which are small enough to fit in the palm of a hand or onto a utility belt, and can fly about 1 km and stay aloft more than 25 minutes. The 18-gram craft has three cameras and even thermal cameras to fly at night.

NASA released the best view of the asteroid (or dwarf planet) Ceres (the largest in the asteroid belt between the orbits of Mars and Jupiter, diameter 945 km, discovered in 1801), which was taken by Dawn spacecraft from a distance of 5,100 km, and shows craters caused by 're-impact'. It reveals small craters caused by the 're-impact' of debris. But the bright spots on the surface of the dwarf planet remain unexplained.

Audi has revealed the fastest self-driving electric car, at the Consumer Electronics Show in Shanghai. It has two electric motors, a top speed of 250 km/h, and reaches 100 km/h in 3.9 seconds. The car uses laser scanners, ultrasonic sensors, radar and video cameras to build up a detailed picture of its surroundings.

More than half of adults believe children today are more stressed, experience less quality family time, and have worse mental and emotional health than in the past generations.

April 11 - two Russian SU-24 Fencer swing-wing jet fighter bombers flew high-speed simulated attack maneuvers against the U.S. Navy guided-missile destroyer USS Donald Cook steaming in the Eastern Baltic Sea, as an example of Baltic buzzing of U.S. Navy warship, in a case lesson in how spheres of influence are enforced. This was the first of a few recent military moves by Russian aircraft flying closely to a U.S. military warship and military surveillance aircraft operating in the Eastern Baltic Sea, near Poland and Lithuania.

April 12 - a Russian KA-27 Helix helicopter flew seven circles, at low altitude around the Donald Cook. Less than an hour later two more Russian SU-24s jets made 11 close-range and low altitude passes over the U.S. destroyer -- as close as 10 m from the ship. The Cook's commanding officer said the low-altitude jet and helicopter passes were unsafe and unprofessional. The Cook had been working together with a Polish military helicopter, and the

Russian flyovers compelled the ship's commander to cease flight operations.

April 14 - a Russian SU-27 jet fighter flew at high speed toward the side of a U.S. RC-135 four-engine reconnaissance aircraft flying over the Baltic Sea. The RC-135 is a specially equipped electronic intelligence (ELINT) aircraft designed to eavesdrop on an adversary's communications, radar, and networking. The Russian jet fighter then closed to within 20 m of the RC-135's wingtip, and conducted a barrel roll starting from the left side of the aircraft, going over the top of the aircraft, and ending up on the right of the aircraft. Like the unarmed simulated attack runs on the destroyer Cook days before, the Su-27's behavior was called unsafe and unprofessional. The U.S. warship and reconnaissance aircraft were operating in international waters and international airspace when the incidents happened.

May 10 – In Boston, USA, the European Food Festival will be back! International professionals will be present and everybody will be sampling tasty foods, wines and beers from France, Germany, England, Switzerland, the Netherlands and Sweden. Lively conversations and great networking opportunities will take place!

Washington's quote: *The Constitution is the guide which I never will abandon.*

341 BC. Aristotle is 43 years old, and he is the tutor of Alexander, 15 year old. Six years later, in 335 BC, inspired by Plato, Aristotle (49) opens his own school, Lyceum, in Athens. Aristotle leaves Athens shortly after the death of Alexander the Great in 323 BC. In 322 BC, Aristotle dies at 62, and Theophrastus (c. 371 – c. 287, in Plato's Academy between 353 BC and 347 BC, then works with Aristotle (13 years older than him), especially in biology, plant biologist) leads the Lyceum, at 49.

Philip II of Macedon completes his annexation of Thrace. Five years later, in 336 BC Philip II is assassinated, at 46, and he is succeeded by his son, 20 years old, who becomes Alexander the Great. In 323 BC, Alexander the Great, 32, dies in Babylon and his huge empire is divided among his successors

Demosthenes delivers his Third Philippic, and he demands resolute action against Philip II. Demosthenes becomes supervisor of the Athenian navy. A grand alliance is organized by Demosthenes against Philip II, which includes Byzantium and former enemies of Athens, such as Thebes. The Athenian Assembly denounces the Peace of Philocrates, which has been signed by both sides 5 years ago, in 346 BC, an action equivalent to a declaration of war by Athens against Macedonia.

The First Samnite War ends with Rome triumphant, and the result is a major acquisition by Rome of the rich land of Campania, with its capital of Capua.

Epicurus is born, future Greek philosopher, founder of Epicureanism (died in 270 BC, at 71).

Aristotle's quote: *The roots of education are bitter, but the fruit is sweet.*

Chapter 5: Lucas philosopher

Commentary on Turing's ``Computing Machinery and Intelligence'' [1]

Turing's aim was to refute claims that aspects of human intelligence were in some mysterious way superior to the artificial intelligence that Turing machines might be programmed to manifest. He sought to do this by proposing a conversational test to distinguish human from artificial intelligence, a test which, he claimed, would by the end of the twentieth century fail to work. And, it must be admitted, it often does fail---but not because machines are so intelligent, but because humans, many of them at least, are so wooden. The underlying question is about the limits of ``algorithmic intelligence'', whether all reasoning is in accordance with some rule or other---whether, that is, to be reasonable is to be acting in accordance with a rule---or whether some exercises of reason go beyond anything covered by antecedent rules. But whether or not this is so, there are many people, bureaucrats, legal clerks, accountants, who are entirely rule-governed, and take care never to do or say anything unless it is in accordance with the rule-book. Turing's Test would classify them with the artificial algorithmic intelligences, not because they were artificial, but because their responses were mechanical.

It is a distinction we are familiar with in ordinary social life. Often we find ourselves having entirely predictable conversations with people who invariably say the correct thing and utter conventional opinions and manifest standard responses; but occasionally we meet someone who has interesting ideas and says things which we had not thought of but which we immediately recognise as right and fitting. Turing parries this variant of Lady Lovelace's objection [p.450.](p.21.){p.56.} by suggesting that ``There is nothing new under the sun'', and that all his thoughts are really unoriginal. But the objection lacks force, as Turing himself admits: ``I do not expect this reply to silence my critic. He will say that. <they>. are due to some creative mental act. .''[p.451.](pp.21-22.){p.57.} But the crucial point is that we do make the distinction, whether or not we sometimes misapply it. We distinguish conversation with Turing's critic, who has a mind of his own, and, when we introduce a topic, can ``go on'', making fresh apposite points, from conversation with someone who produces only programmed responses with nothing individual or original about them. We have the concept of non-algorithmic intelligence.

    Turing says that the argument from creativity leads back to the argument from consciousness, which he considered closed, since those who support it are committed, whether they realise it or not, to solipsism. It was a point easily made in 1950 against the background of the then dominant Verificationist theory of meaning. But meaning is *not* constituted by the method of verification. Many understand Fermat's Last Theorem, though few can fathom Andrew Wiles' proof. The tests of whether a person is conscious are one thing, what it means to say that a person is conscious is another. Meaning is a matter not of tests, but of entailment patterns, of what follows from the ascription, or is inconsistent with it. It would be inconsistent of me to say that you were in great pain, and go on to assert that you were as happy as happy can be; rather, I should show sympathy, and not expect you to be able to think hard about peripheral matters. The nightmarish case of a person paralysed by curare, yet conscious while an operation is performed under an ineffective anaesthetic shows how different the concept of consciousness is from the criteria for its ascription. It is characteristic of consciousness and mental concepts generally that though we often have good grounds for ascribing them, our ascriptions are subject to subsequent withdrawal. It is the same with truth. We often have good grounds for holding that something is true, and quite often are right in doing so, but, apart from some empty tautologies, live with the perpetual possibility of being wrong. This shows that Turing's Test is much less definitive than he thought. Its logic is not the simple, clear logic of deductive argument, but the messier ``dialectical'' logic of *prima facie* arguments and counter-arguments, of objections and rebuttals, inconclusive arguments, and conclusions subject to 'other things being equal' clauses, and the possibility of our having later to emend them. It does not follow that Turing's Test is not good, but it does follow that its application is more difficult, and may involve wider considerations than a simple exchange of conversational gambits.

One feature of consciousness is that a conscious being can be the subject of its own thought. Turing complains that no evidence was offered for this claim, but it seems true, and I think that it opens the door, when we come to think about our own rationality, to certain sorts of reflexive thought and self-referring argument of great importance.

Turing is dismissive of the ``Heads in the Sand'' objection, when the consequences of mechanism are considered and found to be too dreadful. But although we have to be prepared to discover that things are as they are and their consequences will be what they will be, there are good reasons for being chary of throwing over established modes of thought too easily. They may have much going for them, and often have been tried over many generations, and found to be reliable. In particular we should be chary of throwing over the idea of rationality itself. If some theory has as a consequence that we cannot trust our intimations of rationality, then we may well be skeptical of the reasoning that leads us to adopt that theory. It is a very general test of a metaphysical system: what account does it give of itself? Does it cut the ground from underneath the considerations that might incline us to accept it? On an autobiographical note it was considerations of this sort that first led me to think about the self-referential paradoxes of reductive accounts of human reasoning, and ultimately to Gödel's theorem as encapsulating the principle of self-reference in a rigorous way.

Turing allows that there are limitations to algorithmic intelligence, but resists the conclusion that human intelligence is therefore superior. Although Gödel and Turing proved their own theorems, each using principles of inference that went beyond those laid down for the system they were studying, it might be that each was actually an instantiation of some stronger system of algorithmic reasoning. After all, once some original move has been recognised as a right one, it becomes possible to encapsulate it in some definitely formulated rule. It has often happened in the history of the creative arts. Novelty in music, in painting, in literature, is first recognised as original, then generally accepted and copied, and then systematized and standardised, and finally becomes *vieux jeu*. So seeming novelty in human intelligence might be algorithmic in some wider system after all; and, even if not already algorithmic, there would be some machine that could be built incorporating the apparently novel move. So ``our superiority can only be felt on such an occasion in relation to the one machine over which we have secured our petty triumph. There can be no question of triumphing simultaneously over *all* machines. In short, then, there might be men cleverer than any given machine, but then there might be other machines cleverer again, and so on."[p.445.](p.16.){p.52.}

These objections were ones I found it difficult to overcome when I was thinking out my ``Minds, Machines and Gödel" [2] I overcame the first by considering the purported mechanical model of the human's own mind; and I neutralised the second by following the `and so on' up into the transfinite. Douglas Hofstadter [3] is not sure whether the foray into the transfinite secures or refutes my argument, and opines that it refutes it because of the Church-Kleene theorem that ``There is no recursively related notation system which gives a name to every constructive ordinal", which means in the case of Turing's contest between an algorithmic machine and a human mind ``that no algorithmic method can tell how to apply the method of Gödel to all possible kinds of formal system". But the absence of such an algorithmic method is crippling only to an algorithmic intelligence. Only if the human mind were an algorithmic intelligence, would it be unable to keep up the pressure as the contest ascended through ever higher transfinite ordinals. If the mind can *understand* Gödel's theorem, as it seems it can, then it will be able to apply it in novel circumstances not covered by any rule-book, and so out-gun an algorithmic machine, however ordinally complex its Gödelizing operator is.

1. `` Computing Machinery and Intelligence". First published in *Mind*, **49**, 1950; page references to this version are in square brackets thus [p.445.]; reprinted in Alan Ross Anderson, *Minds and Machines*, Englewood Cliffs, N.J., 1964, pp.4-30; page references

to this version are in round brackets thus (p.16.); also in *The Philosophy of Artificial Intelligence*, ed. Margaret Boden, Oxford University Press, 1990. Page references to this version are in round brackets thus {p.52.} Also published under the title ``Can a Machine Think?'', in volume 4 of *The World of Mathematics*, ed. James R. Newman, Simon & Schuster, 1956, pp 2099-2123, which has now been reprinted by Dover in their 2000 edition. It is partially reprinted in Douglas R. Hofstadter and Daniel C. Dennett, *The Mind's I*, Basic Books, 1981.

2. `` Minds, Machines and Gödel'', first published in *Philosophy*, XXXVI, 1961, pp.112-127; reprinted in *The Modeling of Mind*, Kenneth M. Sayre and Frederick J. Crosson, eds., Notre Dame Press, 1963, pp.269-270; and *Minds and Machines*, ed. Alan Ross Anderson, Prentice-Hall, 1954, pp.43-59.

Lucas's perhaps best known paper, where his Gödelian argument is presented, is 'Minds, Machines and Gödel', published in *Philosophy*. He began a lengthy and heated debate over the implications of this argument. Gödel's theorem (which Lucas here expounds and defends) tells us that in any system, complex enough to cope with natural numbers, there are knowable propositions that cannot be proved or deduced within the system. Determinism and the Gödelian theorem are incompatible, and determinism must be rejected. Lucas argues that an automaton cannot represent a mathematician, thus refuting computationalism. These and related themes were developed in Lucas's Gifford Lectures (dialogues themselves), published in *The Nature of Mind* and *The Development of Mind*. Over many years, Lucas has continued to strengthen the Gödelian argument against all-comers. Lucas writes: "Most critics concentrate their fire on ``Minds, Machines and Gödel'', without looking at the fuller statement in *The Freedom of the Will*, which includes the rebuttals first published in ``Satan Stultified''."

3. Douglas Hofstadter, *Gödel, Escher, Bach*, New York, 1979, pp.475-476.

On imagination and creativity

I think the imagination Dennis Hassabis attributed to DeepMind is the ability to look at the problem from a different point of view. Instead of following an algorithm, DeepMind imagined itself as, so to speak, wearing someone else's shoes, and surveying the problem from that different point of view. In order to do this, it is necessary to characterize the problem in a neutral, omni-personal way. This is inherently possible, thanks to the Church-Kleene theorem

Dr. Stockton

Arthur Prior complained that I had been ``slithery"; pressed to explain what that meant, he said that I had not used the bad arguments which he had been expecting and which he could have refuted. Many years later, around 1990, I had another encounter with Miss Anscombe. I had given a talk to the C.S. Lewis Club on Lewis's concept of time, and as I was going, the organizers said Miss Anscombe was coming to their next meeting, and please would I come too. So I did. Miss Anscombe repeated her criticisms of Lewis's argument in Miracles, and I took her up on them. She was old and failing, and I had an easy victory, with members of the club producing the different editions of Miracles, and putting them in front of me so that I could quote exactly what Lewis had actually said. My victory then was as much due to ``gamesmanship" (I cited the Einstein-Podolsky-Rosen argument, which she had never heard of) as Miss Anscombe's had been in the original encounter (in Oxford at the time it was said that one should never play mixed hockey in philosophy). But in my first encounter my victory was on the merits of the case. As a schoolboy I had hit upon a similar argument to refute a materialist position put forward by a rival, and I had long been labouring to make it water-tight. In 1957-58 I went to Princeton to bone up of Gödel's Theorem, and had published an article in 1961 ```Minds, Machines and Gödel" (which still gets over 100 hits a week on my web site). There were many other formulations of essentially the same argument around at the time: I give a list of them on p.174 of my Freedom of the Will, Oxford, 1970. Lewis was giving, briefly, a sound argument disposing of a current objection to the whole enterprise of understanding miracles. Miss Anscombe seized upon his brief exposition and treated it like a fully formulated argument, raising objections which a full account would need to deal with, but which were out of place in the book Lewis had written.

It was one of the clubs I often attended as an undergraduate and after 1951 as a graduate. I think most of my attendances were after Lewis ceased to preside. After I returned to Oxford in 1960 I took a larger part, sometimes presiding. I was a bad chairman, and altogether failed on one occasion, sometime after 1966, when I allowed the evening to be monopolized by Bernard Williams and

David Pears, who had strong personalities and entrenched positions (continuing the argument the next day by telephone, while Bernard was staying with us). All the other would-be participants felt frustrated, and this may have contributed to the demise of the club which was due also to the Student movement. .

    I did not know Miss Aldwinckle well, though she used to attend St Cross Church, where my family went, and though I went to her Memorial Meeting. She found the Oxford Philosophy of that era alien and unintelligible. I remember her once coming to my rooms, and demanding to know what answers Ryle and co. could give to her questions. It was impossible to answer because her questions were ones they did not ask, or even think were worth asking. This was actually a criticism of them, not her. What had happened was that in 1945 there had been a clean sweep of the old ideas, and a new set of ``absolute presuppositions" (as Collingwood would have called them) had been installed in their place. Miss Aldwinckle belonged to the pre-1945 world that Lewis had inhabited, and was a fish out of water in the post-war Oxford Philosophy. As the years passed, Oxford Philosophy gradually became less bigoted. The Socratic Club helped the process of bringing serious philosophical questions back into discussion. It was a pity that the encounter between C. Lewis and Miss Anscombe took place so early. If it had happened later, might have got more support from professional philosophers who could have formulated his arguments in Anscombe-proof fashion, and Lewis might have continued his philosophical writing---which would have been good for philosophers, though bad for the rest of the world, if it had been at the expense of his creative literary work

    On April 3, 2014, Lucas receives an e-mail from Bhupinder Singh Anand, Mumbai, India, regarding an evidence-based argument for Lucas' Gödelian Thesis, in which he writes: "In view of your concluding remarks in "The Gödelian Argument: Turn Over the Page", the following submission to the Fifth International Workshop on Classical Logic and Computation - to be held on July 13, 2014 in Vienna, Austria - might interest you: Title: Algorithmically Verifiable Classical Arithmetical Reasoning, PA Provability, and Algorithmically Computable Finitary Arithmetical

Reasoning: The Evidence-Based Argument for Lucas' Gödelian Thesis."

In late September 2014 Mr. Peter Fekete, a philosophy graduate from Cambridge, visited Lucas, and later Mr. Fekete thanked Lucas for his hospitality, and for the help he offered.

On February 23, 2016, Lucas receives an e-mail from Bhupinder Singh Anand, Mumbai, India, regarding an evidence-based argument for Lucas' Gödelian Thesis, in which he writes: "the journal 'Cognitive Systems Research' has accepted for publication my defense of your Gödelian Thesis: Title: The Truth Assignments That Differentiate Human Reasoning From Mechanistic Reasoning: The Evidence-Based Argument for Lucas' Gödelian Thesis."

Chapter 6: Lucas inventor

Mr. Lucas is a mathematician, a philosopher, and also an inventor. He worked alone on his invention "Gapless Points", for improving conventional railway points (or switch, or turnout). He worked on it sometime ago, and wanted to ask somebody to make a scale model, but that man was always very busy, and John didn't like to bother him. Mr. Lucas mentioned it at a college dinner to a colleague, who told him to ask a certain person to patent it, which was duly done. The original patent lapsed.

A firm based in Malmesbury, Wilts, approached Mr. Lucas, and they met at Oxford. The firm dealt with Chinese Railways, and signed a confidentiality agreement. But then it went silent, saying that there were political difficulties in China concerning the running of the railways. Mr. Lucas harbored deep suspicions of their pirating his design, but in November 2015 he was told by Mr. Andrew McNaughton that there was no sign of his invention having been used in the recently constructed new lines.

Meanwhile, Mr. Lucas has thought of Snugfit, an improvement on the original design, which would have made the Potter's Bar (Hertfordshire, 29 km north of London), crash (in May 2002) impossible. He has had a life-size model made in wood.

Mr. Lucas has it in mind to apply for a new patent, in which the previous design is amended and absorbed in a new version that incorporates Snugfit. But it depends on the availability of time and money.

Mr. Lucas wrote the following captivating details about his invention.
Here is a full account of my Gapless Points.

I cannot remember when the idea of gapless points first occurred to me.
For several years I had it in mind to ask Charles Mangles to make a model, so that I could see what they would be like, and show them to potential manufacturers and railway companies. But Charles lived in Pembroke, and his visits home never coincided with ours, so that that scheme hung fire. Then at the Bodley Dinner in

Merton in March 2009 I found myself sitting next the Master of St Catherine's College (Professor Roger W. Ainsworth), and telling him of my idea. He strongly encouraged me to write to Isis Innovations; and so I wrote, somewhat apologetically as a non-scientist, but having been told to by Professor Ainsworth. Most of the people I dealt with at Isis Innovations were concerned with patenting classical productions---plays and TV shows---but I was introduced to Mr. Adrian Samuels, and began to draft a patent application.

My original idea was to avoid the gaps by having the flanges move up against the pointed nose, as shown in the figure points.jpeg,

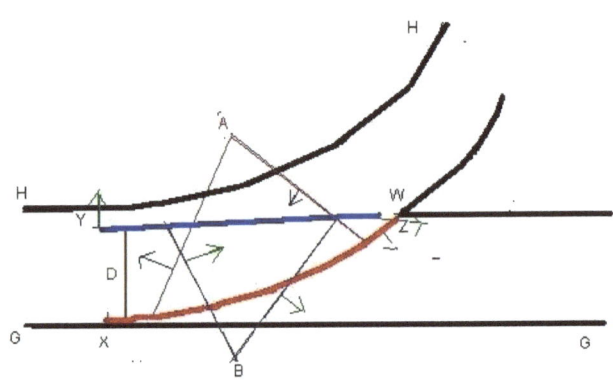

POINTS

Edward and I spent a happy week end making a crude Meccano model. But it was crude, and would not do as a sales model However, on the way back from a party at Sherborne Castles to celebrate our eightieth birthdays, Helen was on the train with my former pupil, Richard Bronk, and told him of the invention and our need to get a better model whereupon Richard volunteered the services of his son Justin, who was a keen modeler. I took the Meccano model to the Bronk's house at Lyme Regis, and Justin made a much more workmanlike model.

As I worked on the draft patent application, I realised that if the flanges were just pressed against the nose, they were still vulnerable to a twisting pressure, and it would be better to cut out the nose altogether, and have them lock onto the small rails which would have met together at the nose.

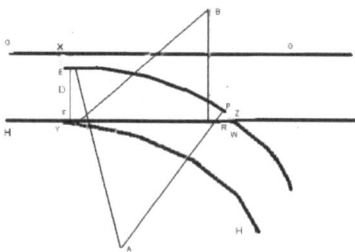

Points5

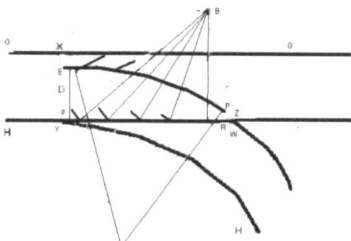

Points6

There was a danger of the flanges twisting under a train's weight---at least one would be slightly curved---; what was needed was that the movable flange should slide into the fixed rail with a snug fit so that it could not in any way become dislodged. This was not something Justin could do, working in metal on a small scale, Instead I found a Mr. Holley, who produced a full-scale model in wood of the movable flange sliding into the fixed rail to make a snug fit.

I now see that the snugfit is a much better approach. It is intuitively evident that it will give smooth ride, and---much more important that it is very safe---the Potters Bar crash could not have happened if the rails locked together in snugfit. The snugfit approach carries with it the geometry of the earlier approach, since the interlocking rails will only slide together if one is moving tangentially. This is not to say that the flanges must be moved by an arm pivoting of a point---though this would be the simplest method, and quite possibly the best when building a new line, and where space was not at a premium. But the flanges could be propelled along guided tracks so as to move along the circumference of a circle even though not a fixed part of that circle.

Snug Fit

One of the great virtues of Gapless Points is that the moving flange fits snugly into the fixed rail, thus ensuring that it cannot twist or come adrift. The disadvantage in the patented design is that the moving flange is long and heavy, requiring much energy to shift it. It is therefore worth exploring possible modifications of the design to avoid this.

Let us consider the case where one outgoing line is straight, and the other curves to the right. We could replace the moving flange by three lengths of straight rail, with the middle length, TU, a fixed section parallel to the left-hand outer fixed rail, and the standard gauge distance away from it, so that it was in line with the right-hand rail of the outgoing straight line and with the right-hand rail of the incoming straight line. At T there would be a pivot and a moveable flange, which could be either tight against the right-hand fixed rail at F, or swung away from it, as on swingnose points.

Lucas working on the models for the points.

    The crucial movement is shown in a diagram. The snugfit moves along a circular arc, centered on B. As it begins its motion it moves in line with the right-hand fixed rail of the outgoing straight line into which it was fitted snugly. Its other end also moves along a circular arc, but that requires it to move away from the fixed rail

TU, which enables the moveable rail to clear the fixed rail. This enables the snugfit to be withdrawn sufficiently to leave a gap for the snugfit of the branching line to engage, and provide a continuous level and twist-free path for the wheels of trains going along the branch. When the points are set for the main line again, the incoming end of the snugfit comes up as a flange tight against the fixed rail in the same way as the whole moveable rail did in the earlier design; and the same double contact and quantum tunneling compound would ensure safety.

Lucas' son Edward working on the models for the points.

Although there would be four, instead of only two, mechanisms, the great reduction of weight in moveable rails having to be shifted, would enable much lighter and cheaper mechanisms to be used. The pivots on which the moving flanges tun would be under less strain than the pivot of a swingnose, because they could be supported by the fixed rail where the flanges come up against it..

Lucas' son Edward and his family on 25 September 2008

Shortly before briefing the patent lawyer, as I researched the patent literature, I came across a rival design, ``Swingnose''. Railtrack had started to install swingnose points in the first decade of the twenty first century, but then had taken them out for safety reasons. I could see why. Swingnose points had a pivot where the two short rails joined, from which a tongue extended away from the two short rails, and could swing so as to come up against one or the other of the two rails leading to the movable flanges.

Clearly the pivot was vulnerable. It would be under considerable strain as a train went over it---though in point of fact, accidents have been few in Europe and Australia where many swingnoses have been installed. It is also worth mentioning that swingnose points have three separate moving parts, compared with only two in gapless points.

Isis Innovation published a flyer, and it attracted some interest.

Railway points (or ``switches") in Great Britain follow the traditional pattern, having a frog with gaps on either side. The gaps give a bumpy ride, cause unnecessary wear on the rails and on the rolling stock. On the continent and in America a swing-nose system is used, which avoids gaps but puts great strain on the pivot of the moveable nose. The system proposed here not only avoids gaps, but has the moving rails lock into the fixed rails so as to provide a firm smooth and reliably safe ride,

The architecture of the system is shown by this schematic diagram. Where space is not a consideration, it would be feasible to have the two flanges actually attached to the pivots A and B, and the two linked together by a cross bar, so that a single movement would switch the points from one position to the other. But in most cases it would be better to have the moveable flanges moved along guides by linked electric motors.

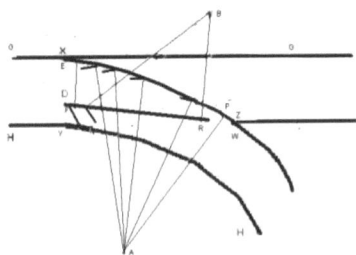

POINTS8

Only two rails would have to move, as opposed to three in the swing-nose system.

Lucas' son Edward and his family on 25 September 2008

There is a full scale model of a key feature, which shows the way the moveable flanges lock into the fixed rails. This is possible, because they come together longitudinally. There is a diagram which shows from the side the moveable flange on the left as it could move to fit onto the fixed rail on the right. It is evident that when locked in, the moveable flange cannot be displaced laterally, and cannot be twisted around its longitudinal axis. The Potter's Bar accident could not have happened if the moveable flange had been locked into the fixed rail in this way.

Some minor detail need to be addressed.

(1) Temperature: long stretches of continuous rail are under tension or stress as they contract or expand with temperature. This would affect the position of the ends of the fixed rails, if they were left unsecured. To avoid this there need to be two bars underneath the sleepers connecting the end of the fixed rail to the opposite outer continuous rail.

(2) Wrong sort of snow: The protruding snout of the ixed rail need to be set at an angle so that if there is snow on the protruding tongue of the moveable flornge, it well be brushed downwards and fall to the ground.

(3) Leaves: leaves could lodge between the thin end of the moveable flange and the fixed rail they come up against: in order to be sure that the moveable flange was tightly against the fixed rail there should be two ceramic or plastic inserts in the moveable flange and the adjoining fixed rail, with a QTC (quantum tunneling composite) switch which would allow current to pass only if the two were tightly pressed together.

(4) False alarms: if both contacts failed, all signals should go to red, but if only one failed, the signal box should be alerted, to send a linesman to clear the leaves; meanwhile trains could be allowed to run, since if there were any serious gap, both QTC contacts would fail.

It is a merit of the design that it can be adapted to cater for higher and higher speeds. Very high speed trains require gentle curves, but a moveable flange can be constructed with high radius of curvate. It will be longer, its weight heavier, and a more powerful and complicated mechanism required to mover it. But in planning for the future, it is a great advantage to be able to accommodate trains being able to diverge from existing track without having to slow down.

With higher speeds and a more complicated mechanism, there might be fears about safety. To ensure that the relevant ange was tightly against the xed rail at X or Y, there could be two ceramic or plastic inserts in the ange and the adjoining xed rail, with a QTC (quantum tunneling composite) switch, which would allow current to pass only of the two were tightly pressed together.

Then if there were any slackness in the system, the circuit would be broken, and all signals would go to red.

A representative of Mouchel came to inspect it, but seemed (to Justin as well as myself) to be wanting only to find fault with it---he went on for a long time about the fact that rails were kept under stress, and we had not made any allowance for that. But it was obvious that the stress could be maintained by having two steel plates underneath the lines each connecting one of the shorter rails to the long one on the opposite side. Much more hopeful was a visit from an English business man who had many business connections with the Chinese Railways. They were building many new lines, and he reckoned would be keen to develop the design and put it into production. He entered into a confidentiality agreement.

Suddenly the Chinese intermediary went off the air, and letters and E-mails went unanswered. I had my suspicions. I wondered whether if I were to fly over China I should see their points all built to my design. But recently I heard from a high-up in HSP2 who had been in China, that he had seen no sign of points built to my design. So it may be just a matter of railway politics in China, where much skullduggery has been going on, and I cherish the hope that some turn of events the Chinese railways will realise they need gapless points, and will be ready to pay me for having thought of them.

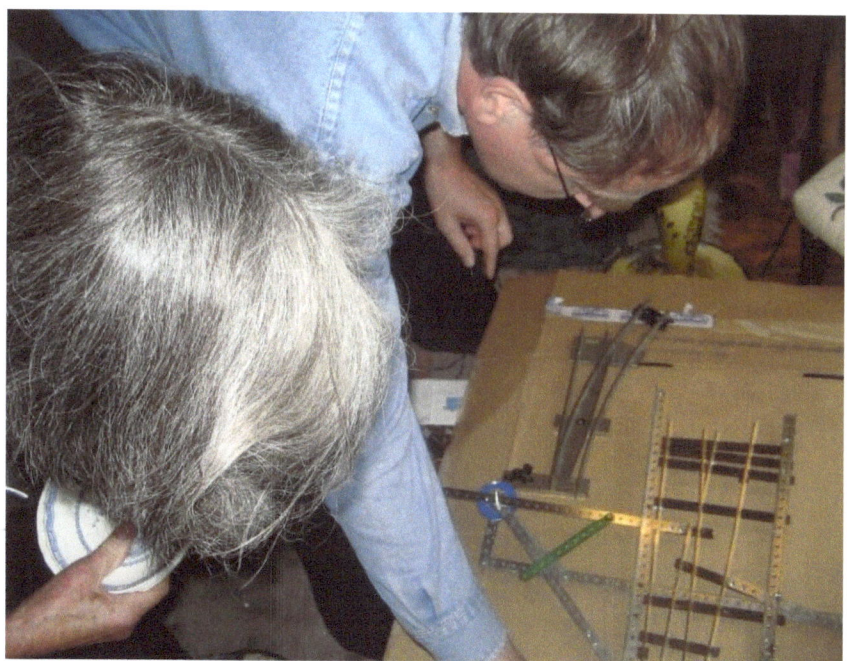

Lucas and his son Edward working on the models for the points.

Gapless Points

Conventional railway points have gaps. The diagram below shows a left-hand point (not drawn to scale) set to direct a train approaching from the left onto the track curving leftwards. The right-hand wheels of the train begin at **X** to be guided along the curved blade marked in red (or purple) and go over a gap to continue at **W**. The curved red blade is rigidly connected to the straight blade (marked in blue) by a cross bar (marked in purple) **D** and another near the gaps, pivoted at **C**. When the points are set to direct trains along the straight, the straight blade, marked in blue, touches the fixed rail **HH** at **Y**, so that the left-hand wheels of the train go along the straight blade and cross the gap to go onto the fixed rail at **Z**.

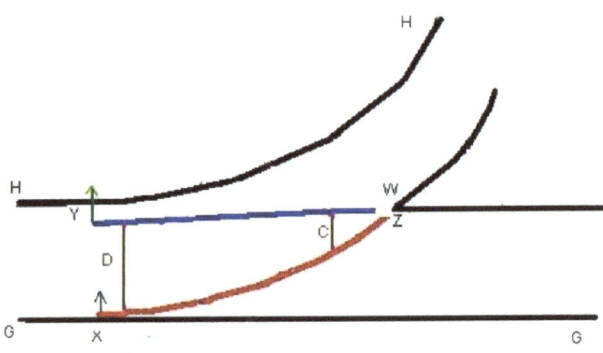

Standard Left-hand Point

There is much wear on the fixed rails at **W** and **Z** and on the wheels of the rolling stock, and passengers are jolted.

The gaps can be eliminated if, instead of both the blades being pivoted at **C**, each is pivoted separately, at **A** and **B** as shown in the figure below. The pivots can be actual, as in the figure, or virtual, with the blades being moved along guides as if they were turning along pivots. For ease of exposition, the design with actual pivots will be given first. Bars, going under the fixed rails **HH** and

GG, connect the curved blade to **A** (marked in light brown), and (marked in light green or pale blue), connect the straight blade to **B**.

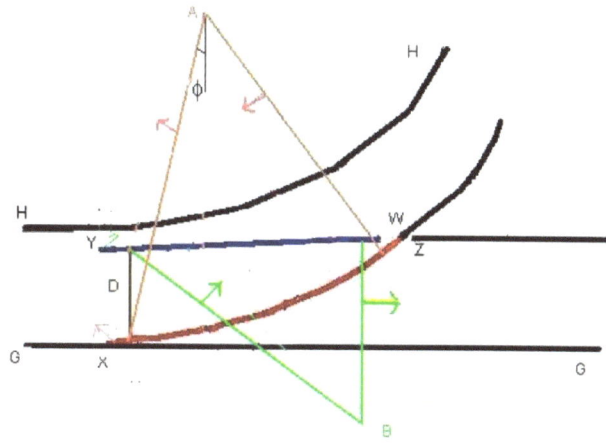

Gapless Left-hand Point

For the sake of clarity the pivots **A** and **B** are drawn well outside the fixed rails. The actual position will depend on the clearances desired and lengths of the blades. The radius of curvature of the curved blade at its **W** end should be the same as that of the fixed track just to the right of **W**; if the radius of curvature is x and if y is the desired gap between the curved blade and **Z**, when the points are set for the train to continue along the straight track, the angular movement around the pivot **A** will be y/x radians. The length of the bar **AX** will be somewhat longer, since the radius of curvature of the blade diminishes towards the **X** end. The angular movement at the tip of the blade at **X** will be correspondingly somewhat larger than y/x, but the important *lateral* movement will be only $\sin\psi$ as large, where ψ is the angle between the bar **AX** and the perpendicular to the fixed line **GG**. This is not a stringent constraint, since

   1. the clearances are only the minimum ones required, and can be exceeded without difficulty;

   2. although it is desirable that the pivot **A** should be on the radius of curvature, it need not be exactly at the centre of curvature.

There is less constraint on the location of **B** for the straight blade, since it can be at any distance from the blade. If the angle between the two bars at B is 45^0, the increased length of **BY** will cancel out the diminished lateral movement of **Y**. Although this is the best design for securing gaplessness, it would be feasible to bring the two pivots much closer in.

Lucas' son Edward working on the models for the points.

The alternative, virtual-pivot, design dispenses with real pivots altogether, and has the blades resting on a number of supports, each of which moves along a circular track centered on a notional pivot **A** or **B**.

When in position, the blade should not simply abut the fixed rail, but should be configured to give a snug fit with the fixed rail. The snug fit can be obtained, because the blunt end of each movable blade moves longitudinally towards and into the configured end of the corresponding fixed rail (hence the desirability of having the pivot **A** at the centre of curvature, or at least on the radius of curvature leading to the blunt end of the blade).

This has three advantages. First, the blunt end of the movable blade rests upon the fixed rail, so that the weight of a passing train is supported directly, and does not put strain on a pivot, or any bit of the movable blade. Second, the movable blade is secured and able to resist any lateral pressure that might arise, particularly when a fast train is beginning to move in a curve. Third, allowance can be made for the movable blade to rise slightly when not engaged, so as to minimize friction when moving as the points are being changed.

To achieve this, the top quarter of the two fixed rails at **W** and **Z** should be cut off (A'B'C'D' in upper diagram below), and each blade should have the bottom three quarters cut off (CDFE), so that the weight of the wheels on the remaining top quarter should be carried by the fixed rail underneath. The edge of the cut-away part of the fixed rails should be beveled, so that if the blade were not lined up exactly right, it would still be able to move into position. The join for the fixed rail and the blade should also be grooved (FDF in bottom left of diagram below to fit over B'A'F'D' in bottom right), diagram below) to secure lateral stability, (it being particularly important to ensure that the lateral force of a high-speed train taking the corner would be met by the fixed rails, and not just the blunt tongue of the curved blade).

The lip **A'B'** of the fixed rail (in top right of diagram below) forces the corresponding slope **AB** on the blade (top left) to come down so that the blade is level with the fixed rail. In order to avoid having the whole weight of a train coming down on the guides, there should be springs lifting each blade a very small distance above the guides, so that when being moved, the blade does not grate on the half chairs, but when there is train on the blades, the blades rests on them, with only a weight approximately equal to the weight of the blade coming down on the guides. When the blade is engaged, the blunt end is brought down by the snug fit to be resting on the half chairs: the top of the tapered end would naturally be slightly above the level of the adjoining fixed rail; it should be ground down to be level. As an incoming train moves onto the tapered end, it will press the blade down until it is resting on its firm supports.

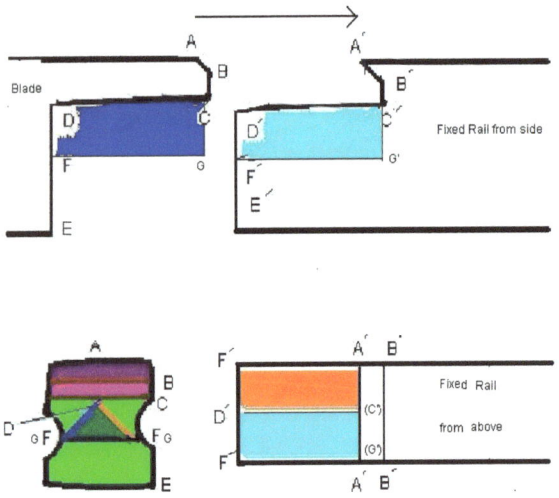

Snug fit between movable blade (left) and fixed rail (right)

Any allowance needed for heat expansion should be accommodated at the **X** and **Y** ends. There are on existing points insets in the fixed rails, so that the tapered ends of the blades can fit snugly in. These insets should be slightly extended towards incoming traffic, so that even in very hot weather the blade would be fitting snugly into the fixed rail. If there were any residual jolting, it would be here.

Safety and Reliability

With higher speeds and a more complicated mechanism, there might be fears about safety. Ice, snow, leaves or dirt might get into the configurations, and prevent a snug fit; or they might build up under the blades and prevent them moving all the way. Or there might be a failure of point motors; or one might fail at the same time as the cross bar **D** was broken. In all except the last case the relevant blade would fail to be tightly next the adjoining fixed rail.

To ensure that the relevant blade was tightly against the fixed rail at **X** or **Y**, there could be two ceramic or plastic inserts in the tapered end of the blade and the adjoining fixed rail, with a QTC (quantum tunneling composite) switch which would allow current to pass only if the two were tightly pressed together. Then if there were any slackness in the system, or if the blunt end of the blade was not quite home, the tapered end of the blade would not be firmly against the fixed rail, so the circuit would be broken, and all signals would be set to go to red. All signals would also be set to go to red if both blades were tight against the adjoining fixed rails.

This arrangement should provide great safety but would be vulnerable to false alarms, for example if a leaf got stuck between the contact on the blade and on the fixed rail. There should therefore be two such contacts. The two contacts should be wired so that if one was not working while the other was, the signals would not be set at danger, but a warning light would go on in the signal box, so that a repair gang could go and see what was amiss. Provided that either current was owing through both contacts or through neither, the signals would be as normal, and no light would show in the signal box.

A second provision against false alarms combined with a timely warning of trouble brewing could be achieved by having, instead of one strong point motor, several| - say four - |weaker ones, with three strong enough to move the blades. Each motor would be monitored, and the signal box warned if any was either using no current or an excessive amount. In some circumstances it would be an economy to have the point motors running of Direct Current, so that simple reversal of polarity would change the points the other way.

In times of snow and ice, if there was little traffic, the points could be altered every few minutes. The incoming blade would scrape and move the snow and the ice forming on the fixed rails, and as it moved it slide down the roof-shaped protruding end of the fixed rail. (But this might not work for the wrong kind of snow!)

.

Gapless Railway Points
John Lucas (Merton College)

Railway Points

Electrofrog point

Issues
_ The gaps results in wear (fixed rails and wheels).
_ Passengers comfort
_ Speed limitations at Bends

Proposed Solution
"A new arrangement of movable rails or flanges in railways points"

Implementation facts and challenges
_ Actual Position depends on clearance and length of flanges
_ Is it OK to have pivots outside existing structure?
_ Obstruction to the movement of flanges

_ Radius of curvature of the flange and lateral force
_ Existing gap and wheel sizes
_ Measure of wear and economics behind it
_ Measure of discomfort (jolt)
_ Heat expansion and Quantum Tunneling Composite
_ Support at frogs

Key Measurements

1. Full length fixed rail North side
2. Full length fixed rail South side
3. Fixed rail to point North side
4. Fixed rail to point South side
5. North gap at point: length width
6. South gap at point: length width
7. Length of North moveable flange
8. Westward continuation of North moveable flange
9. Length of South moveable flange
10. Westward continuation of south moveable flange
11. Gap between flange and fixed rail.
12. Inset on fixed rail to accommodate tapered flange.
13. Length of tapering.
14. Height of rail.
15. Width of rail.
16. Height of concavity
17. Width of concavity
18. Actual gauge (inner)
19. Distance between tracks at East end
20. Clearance on either side.

Chapter 7: Foreign Expeditions

On Wednesday, August 15th, 2001, Lucas received an E-mail with Greetings from Belluno.
Dear Prof. Lucas,
My name is Daniele Casagrande. I suppose this name tells you nothing but I know that, if you are that John Lucas I suppose you are, in 1956 you came, I think for holidays, to a small town in Italy called Belluno (author's note: Belluno is a town in northeast Italy, 100 km north of Venezia (Venice), and 50 km south of Cortina d'Ampezzo).

At that time you lived in a country of the periphery called Gioz (author's note: Gioz is a street and suburb in the north part of Bolzano, 4 km northwest of Belluno) and you became friend of some of the boys of that country. One of that boys is my father, and his name is Marino.

I'm writing to you because some days ago I came in England for holidays and before I left my father told me that if I had gone to Oxford I should have look for a professor named John Lucas and bring to him his greetings.
I didn't come to Oxford but at my return I looked for you in the internet site of Oxford University and found your e-mail.
So:
Many greetings from Belluno from a person you met 45 years ago.

In November I will come again in England, near Reading, for my job, and I would like to have the possibility to meet you personally.
Best regards,
Daniele Casagrande"

On September 1, 1997, Lucas reported to Miss Day:
"Sometime in the 1970s a letter reached the Subfaculty of Philosophy in Oxford from a group of Czech dissident philosophers. I believe it had been held up for a long time at the University Offices before being sent to the Subfaculty. It was read out at a meeting of the Subfaculty, and Dr. K.V. Wilkes, Fellow of St Hilda's, volunteered to make contact with them, and was commissioned to do so on behalf of the Subfaculty. She was the driving force of the whole business. Almost all the credit should go to her.

My own involvement was later, and very small. In February 1980 I was asked to go to Prague for a long weekend, in place of someone else, who had decided not to go. By then a number of philosophers, mostly from Oxford, had been, among them Tony Kenny, Christopher Kirwan and Bill Newton-Smith. Tony Kenny and Bill Newton-Smith had been caught by the Czech authorities, and expelled. So the next in line (whose name I never knew, but he was not from Oxford) had cold feet, and there was a sudden vacancy. I was on sabbatical leave at the time, and so free of hard commitments, and likely to be able to go, if willing. I forget who asked me---it might have been Bill Newton-Smith or Roger Scruton from London, who was much involved. I agreed to go.

I decided to go unpublicly, the object of the exercise being actually to meet and give encouragement to Czech would-be philosophers, not to have a confrontation with the communist authorities. My fifteen-year-old daughter went to London to get me a visa: the application described me as a don, living in Merton Street, employed by Merton, with the purpose of visit being ``cultural". Nothing was untrue, but there was nothing to alert communist officials that I was a university lecturer from Oxford going to have discussions with Czech dissident philosophers.

I took some books with me, purchased with the aid of a grant from, I presume, the Jan Hus foundation. I think there was a Greek New Testament, the psalms in Polish (which I reckoned would be more or less comprehensible in Czechoslovakia), an English translation of Boethius' *Consolations of Philosophy*, copies of my own works, and others I cannot now remember. I took the text of a paper I should read, if occasion arose, to my Czech hosts. It was a version of a paper I had recently read to the Moral Sciences Club in Cambridge on the truth of future contingent propositions---a topic on which I had been working during my sabbatical leave and which ultimately saw the light of day in my The Future; I had used a word processor to change `Cambridge' into `Prague' and `Oxford' into `Brno', in order to make it more appropriate to my audience, but with bizarre results when it came to citing books (see Gilbert Ryle, *Dilemmas*, Prague, 1954 and A.N. Prior, Past, Present and Future, Brno, 1967). I also took for Roger Scruton a long-playing record for a young lady of his acquaintance---I think there was a plan that he would marry her in order to get her an exit permit.

    I was met at Prague airport by Tomas Liska, a tall thin dark-haired student. He shepherded me and looked after me exceedingly well: I only regret that I was not able to do more for him in return when he came to Oxford, and make his time there more of a success. Tomas took me by a circuitous route to some suburb of Prague. Although I could have been put up there, it would have been illegal, and could have caused much trouble if I were caught; so it was decided that I should be booked in to a hotel, and in the evening I was booked into one a few hundred yards North East of the old gate of the Old City. There was a communist *Gauleiter* in the hotel keeping an eye on things, and she scrutinised my passport and asked what `don' meant. I started to explain the Oxford tutorial system without mentioning that it was a university, and she, who no spik much English, did not understand. So I asked `*Parlez vous Francais?*', and she nodded; `*Tous les jeune hommes parlent avec moi et je les ,coute'*, but she did not understand, so I said `*Sprachen Sie Deutsche?*', which again she indicated that she did, and I began `*Alles die Junges sprachen mit mich, und ich . .*' which again left her uncomprehending, so I tried `*Parliamo Italiano?*', and went on `*Tutti i ragazzi parlano con me ed io,*' but still she did not understand what it was to be a don. Meanwhile all the other members of the hotel staff were standing by. I had sensed that they did not like her. What came over to them was not that the inwardness of the Oxford tutorial system was not being explained intelligibly to a Central European outsider, but that the obliging foreign guest was addressing the *Gauleiter* in every available international language and that she could not understand any of them. So she gave up, and I was booked in.

I had breakfast each morning at a 20th century Hapsburg building just north of the old gate, and was waited on by a waitress whom I called the Duchess: she had the look of someone who had been brought down in the world by communism. After a day or so she indicated that she would be very ready to change currency for me. I had already changed some with a taxi driver, but was glad of this facility. I think she was safe, but ought to have been more circumspect, and by the end of my stay was thinking of changing money in Wenceslas Square until warned by my hosts that it would give the authorities just the excuse they were seeking to arrest me.

During the weekend I was taken by Tomas to visit various dissidents. Most of them were night-watchmen or hospital orderlies, as these were the only ones who had access to telephones, on account of their duties. I remember spending some time in the basement of one hospital amid cylinders of nitrous oxide and oxygen, while the message was sent round that Mr. Lucas from Oxford had arrived and would hold a seminar on Monday. They were finding difficult to organize anything, as their last two visitors had been expelled, and their meeting the previous Monday had been broken up by the police. I was very much on the qui vive to see if I was being followed, looking over my back as we went down alleyways to see if anyone was behind us. I empathized with Kafka. In fact I am fairly sure that I had not been detected. The authorities were on the alert, and did in fact catch and expel one philosopher that weekend, but he was a West German, who had been invited by the official university. While I was there I tried to look un-English---so much so that I was asked the way on one occasion. We went past the British Embassy, and Tomas pointed out the spy camera that recorded everyone who went in or out. I had, on advice from the Foreign Office, telephoned the Embassy on arrival, but not giving an eaves-droppable clue to my identity. Just before I left I telephoned again from the airport: this was a mistake---with sufficient effort examination of the passenger lists would have enabled the authorities to work out who it must have been; I should be interested if the files, now open, show that they had.

We were at a bit of a loose end over much of the weekend, owing to the difficulty in assembling an audience. Tomas took me sightseeing, pointing out where there had been a statue of Stalin (or perhaps Lenin) until it had been toppled after a change of regime. He explained to me the different sorts of opposition there were: the Christians, the artists and the disillusioned (or reformist) (ex-) communists. I was taken to the English library at Charles University, which was a focus of dissent. I saw the wall that was built in a time of great unemployment, and manuscripts from the time of Hus, conveying some rather grisly Oxford logic of the Schoolmen---I wondered how far the Bohemian intellectual freedom-fighters of the late Middle Ages made of these logico-linguistic exercises as the gateway to religious liberation---a problem that was later to floor Tomas.

Although it was mostly Tomas who looked after, took me to restaurants, and showed me around, I was also looked after by the girl for whom I had brought the record. Her name was a feminine version of Dvorjak Lenka Dvorkov. She took me to the opera---Mozart, if I remember right. Afterwards, I very properly saw her back to her digs, but then she felt impelled to guide me back to my hotel; and then we agreed in the end to separate midway. Shortly before we did, a police patrol car accosted us, but she was able to deal with them satisfactorily. What I now remember is that we thought it perfectly safe to walk, either together or separately, through the town late at night, our only concern not to be picked up by the police, but with no fear of being mugged.

On one day I found myself at odds with her and Tomas. We had been at the Jewish Synagogue, with its gruesome record of Nazi atrocities. The topic of the Sudeten Germans came up, and I remarked that their expulsion was some sort of requital for the enormities inflicted by the Germans on the Czechs. Tomas and Dvorjak sharply disagreed: the expulsion of the Sudeten Germans had been a crime, and one that had greatly damaged Czechoslovakia. They had originally come at the invitation of the King of Bohemia, and had greatly contributed to the cultural life of Prague in particular and Czechoslovakia generally. Prague had been an international city, the third greatest in the German-speaking world, and now was a provincial backwater.

Dvorjak wanted to escape. After I got back to England, I approached the Airey Foundation, which had been set up in memory of Airey Neave who had been murdered by the IRA (and was an old Mertonian) to obtain funding for her, and entertained fantasies of smuggling her out via Hungary and Yugoslavia (a Foreign Office friend warned me to steer well clear of Bulgaria). But in the end she decided to stick it in Czechoslovakia---I wonder what became of her.

On the Sunday I attended a Protestant church service, which made me feel how German the Czechs were in all but language, and was then taken to meet an old man, whose name escapes me, I am sorry to say, to give him some money from the Jan Hus Foundation, and to talk with him. He was more or less under house arrest, being allowed out for only two hours each day. Tomas and another went in: his rooms were bugged, so they could not tell him by audible words that I was outside, but wrote it down. He came out, and we walked in a nearby park, talking of Seneca and Aristotle's De Anima and other forbidden subjects. There was still the remains of snow in the park, and he was a frail seventy, made to work as a stoker.

On Monday evening I read my paper, sentence by sentence, each being then translated into Czech by Tomas for the first half, and someone else for the second. I wondered whether my audience were much enlightened by what I had to say. My feeling was that it was much more the occasion than the substance that was important. By doing philosophy they were professing freedom---it did not matter that what I was offering was rather technical discussion of difficult dry points: they were the difficult dry points that had been discussed by Aristotle and the Schoolmen, and to be present when they were discussed now was to be in touch both with a long tradition of free enquiry and with the contemporary West.

The previous week's meeting had been broken up by the police, and although care had been taken not to give away the fact that there was to be another meeting, this time to hear a philosopher from Oxford, it was all too likely that there would be a repeat raid. Against that contingency some plans had been laid: someone would telephone a hospital, where there was an outside line, and a message would be telephoned to Oxford within minutes, and could be brought to a meeting of the Subfaculty of philosopher, which would be having its meeting (Monday of Seventh week, 8.15pm until 10.30pm at least), and could pass a resolution condemning the raid in time for the next day's headlines. I had also made an arrangement with my wife, that if I spoke to her on the telephone and was not speaking under duress, I would, somehow or other, bring railways into the conversation: so that if she heard me speak with no mention of trains, she should not believe what she was being told. But in fact there was no raid (though I half remember that there had been another on an artistic exercise that some of those present had been engaged in). My talk went on too long, seeing that it had to be translated sentence by sentence, and we dispersed, emboldened if not enlightened.

The next day I caught a town bus to the airport, not the tourist bus, which was much more expensive. As we approached the airport, I dropped my screwed up ticket on the floor, and was sharply reprimanded by the conductor, who was much put out to discover I was not a native, and apologized: once again, I felt I was in Germany, but a hospitable part of it. I passed through customs--- this time there was nothing they could have taken exception to: although I had many messages, I had not written anything down. Someone in the Departure Lounge wanted to buy my Rubik's cube off me. Another aeroplane full of party officials took off for Moscow. I boarded ours. It taxied down the runway, and took off. An immense sense of release suffused my body, and I began to write down all the messages I had committed to my imperfect memory. Nine and three quarter years later my son, Edward, who had been in Prague covering the velvet revolution, went on to Bucharest, to report on what was happening there for the BBC and the Independent. He was caught by the Rumanian Securitate, and bundled on to a plane going back to Prague. As the plane took off, he too had the same sense of release that I and my colleagues had had: but this time going to Prague, not from it.

My memory after seventeen years may be at fault. There may be still extant a contemporary report I wrote for Merton's Higher Studies Fund, which helped defray the cost. The by-laws allowed it to pay only for exercises that could be described as research, so my report was heavily nuanced in that direction. But it was quite truthful, so far as it went."

On March 17th 2012 Lucas writes:

"It was a wonderful do. After you gave us your very generous present for our eightieth birthdays, I thought of things to do, and on the strength of it, went to Poland, to stay with Richard and his family. But that did not use all that much of it, and, anyhow, was more or less a normal expenditure. I then began to think of the Aurora Borealis. We had seen some of the Wonders of the World---the waterfalls at Iguassu in South America and Niagara, and more recently had journeyed into the Sahara, to see the total eclipse of the Sun. The Northern Lights were a natural next. I toyed with the idea of a one-night expedition from Bristol airport, which was cheap(-ish), but chancy, and would involve either a long drive home or finding a hotel near the airport (I think there aren't any), so left it to a later date. Morar does not like the cold, and I reckoned that Iceland was further south and warmer than Norway; and that autumn would be dark enough and less cold. But no window of opportunity presented itself last autumn, while the newspapers kept telling us that we were at an eleven-year high for the sun-spot cycle that causes the Aurora. So we began to follow up advertisements, and search the web seriously, and reconsidered Norway, but Iceland had other geological delights, whereas Norway offered only igloos, reindeer and snowmobiles, all rather chilly. We settled on Iceland, and I began to look up weather reports, and agonize whether Tromso in Norway would be having less cloud that Keflavik in Iceland.

We set off on Tuesday. We could not go earlier because Edward had a book launch for his Deception: Lies, Spies and how Russia is Duping the West, (and anyhow there would have been a light-polluting full Moon). So, after a meeting at the British Academy, which I am pressuring to publish the details of what its Fellows write, we caught a plane. I had booked seats by windows on the right-hand side so as to see to the north when we were above the clouds---but we weren't. Even at 36,000 feet, we were in thick cloud, and there was nothing to be seen on the ground when we landed at midnight.

The hotel taxi took us to what looked like Didcot power station on a dark December night, with steam billowing out of the cooling towers---which turned out to be small buildings with steam issuing from the ground around them (one we saw next morning was only

25 yards from our hotel room). In Reykjavik the next day the Information office showed us maps of likely Northern Lights and weather charts, which indicated that our hotel was as well placed as anywhere for actually seeing them. Most of Reykjavik is modern, American and ugly, but the old town is picturesque and very small----the Cathedral much smaller than Merton Chapel----somewhat like All Saints on the corner of the Turl and the High). Everyone was extremely helpful: most notably in the bus station, where we, having misjudged our walking speed, arrived just after the bus back had departed, and the receptionist telephoned the bus to wait and sent us off in a car to catch it. Again and again and again we noticed great helpfulness, and although on the whole Iceland is a country for younger and more vigorous holiday-makers, I would strongly recommend it, on this score at least, for the doddery oldies.

The ``Didcot power station" is actually a thermal plant that taps the hot water welling up from the bowels of the earth, and circulates around Iceland. Almost all the houses are heated by it, and supplied with hydroelectric electricity, so that one could have a shower with a good green conscience, knowing that however much water one used, one was not adding any carbon dioxide to the atmosphere. We also bathed in an open-air swimming pool; it was a little bit like the Dead Sea, very salty to taste, though not so nasty, and making it much easier to float in, but warm and in different places at different moments positively hot, sometimes almost too hot; but just as one was beginning to wonder whether it was about to get too hot, it would suddenly change, and a cooler, though still warm, current would sweep in. We must have spent nearly two hours in the pool, before clambering out into the icy air and a ten-yard dash into the changing rooms.

We ate an excellent supper in the hotel, looking out at the evening sky, and a sunset as the haze gave way to cumulus clouds and almost a sun. The conjunction of Venus with Jupiter was clearly visible. After it had got properly dark we went up into the observation tower, and onto the open-air platform, but were disappointed at the general cloudiness. Venus and Jupiter were still visible, but no other stars. There were low clouds on the horizon, some pink, probably from the street lights of Reykjavik, some from the aerodrome lights at Keflavik. But sometimes between them and elsewhere there were greenish clouds, which we were willing to believe were really manifestations of the Aurora. With the eye of faith we were seeing the Aurora, and persisted, the air being cold, but not bitterly so. The greenness faded, but reappeared elsewhere, and faith strengthened. Both increased, and finally became indubitable, when there were streaks coming upwards from the North, like beams of light in a dark room, or a bundle of different grasses held firmly in a hand. Several different versions appeared and faded, and finally we decided to go to bed, it being well after midnight, and our being in no doubt that we had really seen the Northern Lights, the main object of our journey.

The next morning we booked a half-day excursion to visit the geysers on Helen's recommendation (she also had told us to pack swimming clothes which we had not thought of ourselves). It was a brilliantly clear sunny day, showing up the snow-clad countryside in dazzling white. In the distance were high mountains, nearer often a flattish plain with conical hillocks (?volcano-ettes?), reminiscent of the pit heaps in County Durham, We got to the geysers, bought a sandwich, walked up past a little geyser, with water boiling furiously in a hole rather bigger than a marmalade pan, and then approached the great geyser as it erupted, sending clouds of water and steam fifty or a hundred feet into the air. There were several smaller busts immediately after, and many more as we ate our sandwiches sitting on a bench with wisps of steam wafting from many places in the ground around us. There was a fence to prevent us getting too close, but we went up to the fence to get a better look, but whichever side we went to the wind changed and blew steam to envelop us and prevent our seeing anything. I was still there at the next eruption, and had a hot shower, not enough to soak or hurt me, but enough to give a distinctly bedraggled appearance.

The next stop was an enormous waterfall I had never heard of. Not as big as Niagara or Iguassu, but in that league: a lake cascading over a cliff and then going over a further fall to disappear from sight into a deep canyon. We had not got our camera to hand but a kind couple took a picture for us which they will send us by E-mail when they get home. We went back via the rift valley where the Eurasian and North American tectonic plates meet. In it was the place where the Icelanders used to have their annual Parliament, lasting three weeks, in which all disputes were settled after they had heard all the laws being recited from memory. (Would that all our laws today were so succinct that they all could be recited from memory by one man!)

We had high hopes of a clear sky and better sighting of the Northern Lights, but as we got nearer our hotel, the sky clouded and it began to snow. We comforted ourselves that we had already definitely seen them, and had also swum in hot water and seen the Great Geyser in action, but remained downcast throughout supper, and having checked in for our flight home and paid the bill, and asked to be rung up if the Aurora appeared, went back to our room to pack. I did not feel like another shower, even though totally green. I went up to the look out, but it was still snowing, laid down in my clothes, went to look again, still snowing, and finally gave in, and went to bed. I woke again around two o'clock, could not get back to sleep, and draping myself in a towel, crept out into the passage and looked out: only a few flakes falling. Went back, dressed, and went to the observation tower. Bitter wind, rails encrusted by snow, but partly clear sky, though no Aurora. Morar had woken, in spite of my stealth, and was looking out of the window to see what I was up to. I came back, and confessed to failure, but kept my clothes on and dozed in a chair. I looked out again, no flakes fluttering down, said I was going to try again and would come back if there was anything to be seen. There was. Not much, but definitely something. I made haste to come down, tell Morar and come back again. She soon came, but it had faded sooner. But there was green to be seen, and then it strengthened, and faded. It was very cold, and it seemed sensible to go inside, but nothing could be seen from inside because of reflections in the glass of the windows.

We went out again, and could see something though not much, and again it faded, and again we thought to go back to bed, but as we took one last look, it got stronger, and we stayed until it had almost gone; once again it seemed time to go in, and the quickly a new arch appeared, starting on the Eastern horizon, and stretching right overhead, and then curling round to the North, like a bishop's crozier laid flat. It strengthened and shimmered, sometimes looking like pleated clothing rustling in the wind. It was not as spectacular as the photographs, but on the tour we had talked with someone who had seen it the night before and she said that when a friend who had photographed it with a time exposure showed her the photograph, she would not recognize it as the one she had seen. Anyhow, ours was spectacular enough. We have come back green, throughout, not only in our outward washing but in our inner memories.

Memoirs about Lucas

Professor Robin Attfield

(1) I was a student of Greats (Literae Humaniores) at Oxford between 1960 and 1964, and began studying philosophy in the second half of this period (1962-4). One of the more striking weekly events (of probably 1963) consisted in a series of dialogues between J.R. Lucas and Alasdair MacIntyre, conducted in one of the halls of the Oxford Examination Schools building. This striking duo would walk in, chatting amicably, set up their reel-to-reel tape recorder, and then engage in fierce debate about Plato's 'Republic', with MacIntyre berating Plato and Lucas ingeniously defending him. After nearly an hour of these exchanges, these two philosophers would round off their dialogue, and walk off again in apparent total amity, carrying their tape-recorder as they went.

(2) After I had published an encyclopedia entry about John Lucas and his contribution to philosophy in 2002, he invited my wife and me to a public re-enactment of the Huxley-Wilberforce debate, which he staged at (I think) a British Academy event in Kensington, London. Lucas played the part of Wilberforce, and a distinguished female academic took the role of Huxley. To some degree this was an updated dialogue, at the same time as a re-enactment, with Lucas giving Bishop Wilberforce lines that he could or should have uttered, whether he actually did or not (rather along the lines of the speeches in Thucydides). He also received us both with extreme courtesy beforehand, telling my wife that he had cause to be very grateful to her husband.

(3) During the year after my retirement in 2009, I was granted funding by the Ian Ramsey Centre of Oxford University for participation in a project on philosophical aspects of the cognitive science of religion, and John Lucas was one of three consultants that I visited for assistance with writing some related essays. So in February 2010 I drove from Cardiff to visit John and his wife in their

village home in rural Somerset. They received me hospitably, and we shared in a fine lunch. Afterwards, John and I sat on either side of a log fire, and John suggested that the problematic but crucial paragraph should be divided and inverted. This did the trick, as the people who had raised problems with this passage raised problems no longer. The essay was published sometime later in an Ashgate volume entitled 'The Roots of Religion", edited by Roger Trigg and Justin Barrett. I remain deeply grateful to John for his help.

Robin Attfield, 'J.R. Lucas', *Dictionary of Twentieth-Century British Philosophers* (2 vols.), ed. Stuart Brown, Bristol: Thoemmes Continuum, 2005, vol. I, 586-90; ISBN 1-84371-096-X

Robin Attfield, 'Lucas, John Randolph', in *Cambridge Dictionary of Philosophy*, third edition, New York: Cambridge University Press, 2015, pp. 614-15.

Priscilla Dobbs

Early memories of JRL from cousins Priscilla & Evelyn Dobbs

Re: our much loved cousin John. Our mothers were sisters & the families have always been in close touch. Our mother was John's Godmother

Our first awareness of John would have been when he was Winchester College & used to cycle out to King's Somborne a few miles away to visit our family-consisting of my parents, my sister, Evelyn (b1942) & myself (b 1940) During the war there was petrol rationing but we remember when the 2 families met for a picnic in or near Winchester. John's parents must have motored from Durham in Old England the 1926 Humber *which John later inherited. This was the occasion when John taught us to eat cherries by sucking them into our mouths via the stalk. Also we probably practiced spitting out the stones & used bunches of cherries as 'earrings'.

John first featured largely in our lives when he came up to Oxford as an undergraduate. In 1946 our family moved to Iffley Rectory (2miles from Oxford) whereas John's was still in Durham. Petrol rationing continued so Iffley was a 'home from home' for John. He & his family celebrated his 21st birthday there & his sisters & friends stayed for College Balls. It was a treat for us to stay up late & 'help' them get dressed. My sister, Evelyn & I (aged 4 & 6 onwards) used to love his visits & the stories which came from the top of his head. (a 20th Charles Dodgson ?) Evelyn remembers a solemn wedding ceremony between her (aged 4ish) & John which took place in our nursery .Not sure who took it but our father was a vicar so we knew the score. John was responsible for our early education in philosophy/logic. He used to tease us that 2 x 3 =7 (& no doubt proved it) Evelyn remembers dancing up & down with rage. She KNEW it was 6 because I had told her. John has always been brilliant at explaining anything to anyone at the appropriate level & vocabulary. (He was recently consulted about an unusual rainbow experience by my sister) John's visits to Iffley Rectory were often on Silly Point, the motor bike which gave him the freedom to roam beyond the university confines.

Sometimes we would walk along the towpath towards Oxford & John wove stories & would tell us about the College Barges, colours & Oxford traditions. This is when the Mildred stories started -an ongoing saga featuring an Oxford cow called Mildred & all the adventures & experiences she had. (Later there was a younger more flighty cow called Matilda) Not many undergraduates would invite their young cousins onto the Balliol barge during Eights Week & keep them entertained with stories about a mythical cow while cheering on the Balliol Eight. John continued to keep us posted about Mildred's doings for many yrs. On one occasion a post-card told us that Mildred had been awarded the OBE. Unfortunately that led to the assumption that this referred to another older family member, also called Mildred (& rather more eligible) One (? or more) Mildred story later appeared in a handwritten blue note book which lived in our 'toy cupboard'. Sadly although we would never have knowingly discarded it, several moves later it has disappeared.

As children we used to visit John at Balliol & Merton where he would invite us to tea, sometimes, with another junior friend. Tea involved the ceremony of meringues, scooping them out & inserting cream with a silver spoon. The room (Balliol) was full of books but Lewis & Short/Liddell & Scott or similar served as a table. One occasion that stands out was hurling meringues into the quad ('Fellows' Quad at Merton) to the astonishment of people passing through .Not that that would bother John. We then collected them to eat-all the more fun because we had foraged for them.

We left Iffley in 1959 so John was in Oxford during most of our childhood. In 1961 Evelyn returned to Oxford as an undergraduate so the tables were turned & she always found a warm welcome with John & Morar in Rose Lane/Grove cottage.

John was unusual (? unique) in that as a young man embarking on a starrily academic career he had the time & imagination for his young cousins at that stage of his life. But of course in John's case his huge brain is matched by a huge heart & the ability to empathise with people of any age.

He has always been strongly family minded .Over the years our as part of his extended family we have all been the beneficiariesof his generosity: invitations to special occasions/lectures/book launches. Unlike many men, he remembers important anniversaries. He never forgot our mother's birthday & in old age, especially, she appreciated that he provided mental fodder in the shape of books & practical help with anything that needed fixing.

We have of course known John all our lives & are in close contact. He continues to look after & entertain his young(er) cousins & can relied upon for an explanation of any subject under the sun.

Priscilla Dobbs   Jan 2016

Christopher Sykes

I have come across your wonderfully friendly and interesting website and I thought I would send you a friendly (and, I hope, interesting) message. You were at my Merton interview in 1964, and as I was given a place to read English, I think the first thing I should do is to thank you. My tutor was John Jones and although I fear I let him down academically (I married my Danish wife Lotte in my second year and we had a son shortly after), I was left with an enduring love of literature and I would also like to think that my later life made good use of what I was taught at Oxford.

After a couple of frustrating but highly entertaining years teaching at a 'Decline and Fall' kind of private school near the summit of Leith Hill in Surrey, I joined the BBC as a researcher in 1970 and I have been making television documentaries ever since, some of them about subjects not so far from some of your many interests. I made a biographical programme about Alan Turing in 1992, another about Hardy and Ramanujan, and I was lucky enough to get to know Richard Feynman quite well and to make a number of programmes with and about him. The first and best one is called 'The Pleasure of Finding Things Out' and consists of Feynman sitting in an armchair and talking for fifty minutes about himself and science - if you have never seen it and have a DVD player, I would be delighted to send you a copy.

I hope you won't think me impertinent for writing to you in this way. Although we never knew each other, I remember you well. Best wishes.

Conclusions

Lucas's achievements include his pioneering the Oxford Joint Honour Schools of Mathematics and Philosophy and of Physics and Philosophy. Pre-eminent among the multiplicity of his philosophical contributions and insights have been his influential work on time (as in *A Treatise on Time and Space* and in *The Future*), and on realism (as in *Spacetime and Electromagnetism*) and, more particularly, the Gödelian argument, which continues to be widely debated.

Lucas has made major contributions to the philosophies of action, mind, religion, science, mathematics, logic, probability, and economics, to ancient philosophy, and moral and political philosophy. He also helped found the Oxford Consumer Group.

The revival of the philosophy of religion also owes much to him. Lucas is an author with diverse teaching and research interests, and he has written on the philosophy of mathematics, especially the implications of Gödel's incompleteness theorem, the philosophy of mind, free will and determinism, the philosophy of science including two books on physics coauthored with Peter E. Hodgson, causality, political philosophy, ethics and business ethics, and the philosophy of religion.

Lucas writes: "I played a part in the British Consumer Movement, and by going to an Annual General Meeting of the British Motor Corporation, forced them to abandon some devious practices to deprive purchasers of their legal rights.

I helped found the Oxford Consumers' Group, and was their first Chairman.

Much later I had a go at British Telecom to get them to deliver telegrams promptly (instead of just putting them in the mail!).

I have one son who is a journalist for the *Economist*, and was until recently their correspondent in Moscow; and another who is a businessman in Poland---bringing Western technology to an ex-Communist country; and a daughter who is a doctor.

I think you could describe me as a dyed-in-the-wool traditional Englishman.

I used to be rung up in the afternoon G.M.T, by New York stockbrokers wanting me to lose money on the New York Stock Exchange. I think they must have got my name from *Who's Who?*, and thought I must therefore be very rich. I used to explain that I was an old-age pensioner, and had not got much money to lose, but would anyhow wait until after the crash before buying their shares. But in fact I am still waiting, because I think the market has still some way to fall---the reason being that what makes business tick is not profits for shareholders, but service for customers."

Sayings

Generosity is one of the remaining pleasures of old age.

Worckahol is the curse of the thinking classes.

``The hungry wolves looked up and were not fed'' (to Theodore Wade-Gery, reporting on Quine's session with the Oxford Philosophical Society the previous night.)

I have been prescribed beauty cream on the NHS because it says in the bible ``How beautiful are the feet'' (told to group of college secretaries in the Old Bank Inn, Magpie Lane).

``The best is the enemy of the good'' (advice given to graduate students at Corpus, Cambridge, who needed to get shot of their theses, and widen their horizons.)

``The effortless inferiority of the non-Balliol non-man'' (speech at 1976? St Cath's night dinner in Balliol.)

``I phile lots of paeds, but don't erast any''.

``I am a man more kissed against than kissing,'' (said allegedly to Ralph Townsend in St Cross Church, and actually to Peter Cornwall in Catte Street, opposite Hertford College.)

``Our friends in the Roman Catholic Church give good answers to bad questions'' University Sermon 197* in St Mary's on the Eucharist.

``Christianity is a religion of failure---not unredeemed failure, but failure none the less''.

Failure leads us to reassess our priorities, and may make us realise that the goals we had been aiming at were not worth pursuing.

``Pilate was not best pleased to be disturbed at an ungodly hour by a bunch of ecclesiastics wanting him to kill someone''.

``You in America have twice-born Christians, but only in England do we have twice-dead atheists'' (said to Dana Scott on the occasion of A.J. Ayer's second death.)

That death, when it comes, should come no longer as an enemy, but not yet as a friend.

If, after my death, I wake up in the next world, I shall be pleasantly surprised.

If you seek truth, you perpetually expose yourself to being wrong.

Chapter 8: Autobiography of Old England

or

One for the Road

I was born on December 5th, 1927, when I left the Humber factory in Coventry, and was baptized on April 24th, 1928, when I was first licensed, and bought by the Misses Peaks, who lived in Guildford.

I joined the Lucas family in the early 30s, when the Reverend E.de G. Lucas, who had been a slum priest in South London moved to be Rector of St Nicolas, Guildford, in 1930, and the Misses Peaks told the Rector that they were buying a new car. The Rector did not preach them a sermon on carbon emissions, and expressed polite interest. That is not the point, they said. We shall be trading in our old car, but will only get a nominal discount for it. How would it be if we traded in your car, which, if you will excuse our saying, it is much less good than our old one, which you can have instead? (Master John, as he then was, remembered the Misses Peaks, as three very old ladies (they were in their thirties)).

Since then I have been part of the Lucas family, watching how the younger ones grew larger, and making it an increasingly tight fit to get them all in. I remember how Master John became able to reach the starter button with his foot, and one day succeeded in pressing it while his father was in the Rectory, getting some luggage. He came rushing out to see what was happening to his car and his son. Thirty years later I was outside Castle Cary station, where Mr. John, as he had become, was bringing Master Edward from London to stay at Lambrook. Master Edward was eyeing the starter button with intent; but his father read his mind, and forestalled any repeat of his own misdemeanour.

Sometimes we would be on a Roman road, near Salisbury, where Mrs. Lucas' father was Dean, or Chichester, where he had a holiday house. Roman roads were very straight, and easy to bowl along at a speed between 45 and 55 miles per hour, which suited me well; and if not too hilly, allowed the hand throttle to be used, giving the right foot a welcome rest. On flat Roman roads we once or twice went up to 60 mph. Master John was thrilled, and I was happy to put a spurt on to please him. But 60 mph is too fast for continuous driving, and it was my undoing in 1965 when Mr. John was speeding to arrive in time to see Churchill's funeral on the television, and I broke one of my valves. Fortunately it turned out that there was a spare set, which had been made long before, because it was then thought that the valves would soon need to be replaced. I now acknowledge that, since I am a family, not a racing, car, that 60 mph is above my station in life.

The car.

I was subjected to various alterations in the 1930s, because the government would keep passing laws. I had to have two plastic signals affixed to each side of my windscreen to indicate if we were going to turn. Later the fashion changed, and Mr. John used them to fix winking lights, which had become de rigueur

Also in the 1930s, again as a result of nannying by the government, I had a nasty operation on my headlights, so that they could be dipped if a car was coming the other way. This was done pneumatically, and a plunger was put on my dashboard next to the starter. But it was shiny black plastic, and did not look at all real. What with that and a black switch for the indicators and a new driver for the windscreen wipers, I was looking a fair mess by the time I was re-bored and re-painted.

But there were compensations. I went to the South of France. A rich parishioner decided that the dear Rector and his wife needed a proper holiday---without their children---and that they should go to the South of France. So we went. And returned, having clocked up thousands of miles. (My milometer only goes up to 25,000---I think it has been round twice).

In 1939 I moved to Durham. The Reverend E.de G. Lucas had been appointed Archdeacon of Durham, and I was proud to convey him as he performed Archidiaconal functions in the County Palatine. I was one of the very few cars allowed to go on Prebends Bridge to cross the river Wear. Luckily I never got stuck on the bridge. There was a continuous gradient from both the Archdeaconry and my garage, and occasionally, when I had difficulty in starting, I would be pushed to start rolling downhill with the gears in third, and the clutch being let out and in to turn the engine. It always worked, I am glad to say---it would have been shaming to be rescued from there.

I did on occasion have to be rescued. The autovac, was unreliable and could cause trouble at inconvenient times. One embarrassing time was when the Master and Mistress were going South from Scarborough where the Mistress had given out the prizes at the Sports Day of Master Paul. Even worse when the same thing happened, as I was transporting them from Winchester via Iffley to Durham and we came to a halt on a roundabout in the middle of Leicester - horrors - just outside---HORROR of HORRORS---the PRISON!

The autovac gave out again at the end of our Durham days, when we were on the Fosse Way. This time it had to be replaced. But I still miss my autovac. It is true that I sometimes had to use the starter a lot before there was enough petrol in the carburetor to make the engine fire but that was a problem anyhow. To get a quick start, Mr. John would squirt a little ether into one of my cylinders. It worked a treat, so much so that I became addicted. Humans had become addicted too, and when Mr. John wanted to buy some more, he was told that it could no longer be bought without authorisation.

So he wrote out an authorisation for him to buy solvent ether, signing it rather grandly ``J.R. Lucas, MA, Fellow of Merton College, Oxford" which was accepted as suitably authoritative. My autovac was replaced by an electric petrol pump, which has been a trouble ever since. It once gave out, to my intense embarrassment, in the car park of Windsor Castle, and Mr. John had to do some creative mechanics to get it going again.

The engine of the car.

That reminds me of the saddest moment of my life. We were again going to Windsor for a meeting at St Georges, and as I was approaching Slough, I saw the Castle on fire. I was devastated. What would become of England, if Windsor Castle burnt down? Thankfully the fire was put out, and the damage, though terrible, was limited.

Besides my autovac, I lost my magneto, which was replaced by coil---again a cause of trouble on account of its unreliability. But it was replaced by a magneto again during an uncomfortable year at Leeds, where I had to live out of doors, exposed to the elements. The magneto was an improvement, but it lacked the facility for advancing or retarding the spark. Normally in the good old days, the Reverend E.de G. Lucas would have the hand controls at five past six, but would retard the spark if I was labouring on a hill, or if he was going to start me by swinging the engine with the starting handle. In recent years Mr. John has had to change down more frequently, and has altogether given up starting my engine by swinging it.

I have almost expunged from my memory a most undignified era when I was out of action, and was raised up on bricks so as not to damage my tires. This indignity I have almost expunged from my memory, but for the sake of completeness I must mention it. I celebrated the end of the war by going to Consett, and achieved 45 mph (at which speed my needle is exactly vertical) on the way back to Durham down a long straight gentle slope.

It was at that period that I got my name. I pride myself on having been part of a benign anomaly in the English Constitution. In 1945 there was a General Election, and the two Houses of Convocation, one for each Province of the Established Church, were deemed to be part of Parliament and were dissolved with the other elected House. The Master was a member of the Northern Convocation, *ex officio*, by reason of being an Archdeacon. He was therefore granted 19 gallons extra of petrol so as to be able to canvas his supposed constituents. This meant that we could go to visit Hexham, which has a jolly good abbey (though not as good as Durham Cathedral). While I was parked outside, the Archdeacon was walking behind two workmen further down the street, and overheard one of them saying to the other ``My! Look at that piece of Old England''', and I have been called that ever since. Later that day we were met by ironic cheers from a crowd returning from an event. In my back was Eric James, who had been Master John's chemistry master, and was going to be High Master of Manchester Grammar School. He stood up, and started bowing to them, and the crowd, having seen many films of triumphant entries into Paris, Brussels and Amsterdam, concluded that he really was someone important cheered still, but respectfully. They were right. Later, as Sir Eric James, he helped found the University of York, and later still, as Lord James of Rusholme, he used to go up to the House of Lords ``in order to meet my former pupils". It was tight fit: besides three in the back, there were three in the front, because the future

Lady James was very thin, and could be squeezed in next the driver. (Of course, I have carried many more. Once in Leeds I had fourteen, but that was too much for my springs, so that my back mudguards were almost scraping the tires. Once on Shotover Hill, Oxford, I had eight boys from New College School for a birthday party. A police van drew up, and was prepared to be disapproving, but after being shown that my indicator lights were in working order, went away, satisfied.)

The engine of the car.

Besides the time in the 1930s, I was re-bored and re-painted after the war, and again in 1961, when Mr. John was getting married. Instead of Humber mole, which had been originally chosen because it did not show the muddy splashes from the roads, I was painted blue---I would have been red, if Mr. John had had another £5 to hand. The remarkable thing was that Mrs. John already knew how to double declutch, and change down smoothly, having learnt to drive a Bull Nosed Morris, when she was only nine, which she could do, as the roads in Savernake Forest were not public highways. She had to sit on a petrol tin, in order to see, with another petrol tin behind her, so that she could reach the pedals. I was very proud to be driven by the only bride in the country who on her wedding day was able to double declutch and change down. I had plenty of opportunity during the following year, to notice how well she did it, when she was driving on her own, going to Savernake for maternity check-ups, when Master Edward was on the way.

In the good old days, the Rector used to condition my leatherwork with Mars oil, but more recently time has taken its toll. A large patch was put on, not very successfully, and many cracks have appeared. I have many other scars. Long ago a no-good garage in Sunderland could not be bothered to find the handle of the right hand back door, and just cut off the end and put a stub on it. One sidelight has been replaced with an ugly modern one. The windshield is missing. It was much used in Guildford days on the way back from the sea when those in the back were liable to feel the cold. But it was taken off in Durham---there was no opportunity of going to the sea---and got left behind when we moved down South. And the old jack has gone. But not all changes are bad. I now have seat belts in the front. These date from Mr. John's being the first at the scene of an accident, where a passenger had been thrown through the windscreen. Safety is more important than authenticity. In some of my windows the talc has been replaced with perspex. Again, I cannot deny that it is an improvement. The talc was yellow, difficult to see through, and cracked easily. Although old, I am really modern-minded, and aim to keep abreast of the times with respect to convenience as well as to safety.

I sometimes celebrate. On the fortieth anniversary of my baptism, Mr. John's sister, now Mrs. Ann Cuming, baked a chocolate cake which she and Mr. John ate with relish, and Mr. John put a bottle of beer in my radiator. He did the same for my seventieth birthday, and tied balloons to my hood, and drove round South Petherton with a notice ``I am seventy today". Two days later he received a letter from the former Vicar of East Lambrook, who had been told that Mr. John was seventy, which of course he wasn't, as he always has been younger than me. Apart from these, I don't party much. Most of the cars of my age have girls' names, and tend to be flighty and unreliable. I have a deep male horn, as befits a car that prides itself on its reliability. (My horn once got stuck, and sounded continuously all the way up Northumberland Street in Newcastle to my great embarrassment. Since then I have realised that silence is often golden, and I sound it as little as I can.).

I discovered my early history by accident. (Nobody remembers being born, and the date of one's birthday is known only at second hand.) I was at Northdown Farm, an apple farm near Haslebury Plucknett, which we often used to visit. The owners were sheltering a man who had been turned out of his house, and was at the farm with all his possessions, which included his grandfather's business records. His grandfather had owned a garage in Portsmouth Road, Guildford. After examining my engine number, he was able to track me from the day I arrived from the factory in Coventry to the day I departed in the Misses Peaks' possession.

My life story is almost complete. There is little to record from the last few years, with Mr. John's failing health being matched by my own decrepitude. I began to have trouble with my starter motor, and a neighbour, Mr. Daniel took it off and had it skimmed. It is now on again, but he says that my wiring, like varicose veins in humans, is worn out and dangerous; and that I need a new owner, and cars like me sell for £25,000 (I was once stopped in Yorkshire by someone who wanted to buy me for £2,000, but that was in 1959 before the great inflation.) But instead of being sold to a stranger, I was given to Dave and Sheila Wright as a Thank You for their years of looking after Deborah. I now live at Chard, and often go to shows and rallies. Dave and Sheila want to do me up, to match the other Humbers, but their daughter, Helen, wants to keep me as I was at the Lucases, a working car of workaday appearance. Either way I shall have a fulfilling life.

(Notes : Bull Nosed Morris (in Cowley and Oxford forms, it was one of the most popular and successful of all British cars, over 168,000 being built between 1913 and 1926).

Savernake Forest (4,500 private acres on a plateau between Marlborough and Great Bedwyn in Wiltshire, 100 km west of London))

J. R. Lucas around 1965

J. R. Lucas was invited in 2006, at the International Conference "John Stuart Mill, 1806 – 2006", Faculty of Philosophy, University of Bucharest, Romania, celebrating two hundred years from the birth (on May 20, 1806, in Pentonville, on the northern fringe of Central London, United Kingdom) of John Stuart Mill, philosopher, political economist and civil servant (died on May 8, 1873, just 12 days before his 67th birthday, in Avignon (539 BC), a city in southeastern France's Provence region, 100 km northwest of Marseille and 280 km southeast of Geneva (Switzerland), on the Rhône River (813 km, originates in the Swiss Alps, from the Rhône Glacier (2,208 m, in the canton of Valais), passes through Lake Geneva, then Lyon, with the mouth in the Carmargue delta, flowing into the Mediterranean Sea, 40 km west of Marseille). From 1309 to 1377, it was the seat of the Catholic popes, and remained under papal rule until becoming part of France in 1791. Its center, surrounded by medieval stone ramparts, contains the massive Palais des Papes (1316) and remains of the Saint-Bénezet Bridge, also known as Pont d'Avignon (1185, 900 m, in 1669 a catastrophic flood swept away much of the structure, only 4 of the initial 22 arches remain, the very famous French song "Sur le Pont d'Avignon" dates back to around 1450)).

J. R. Lucas on November 3, 2006, at the International Conference "John Stuart Mill, 1806 – 2006".

J. R. Lucas around 1990.

www.ingramcontent.com/pod-product-compliance
Lightning Source LLC
Chambersburg PA
CBHW041429300426

44114CB00002B/13